KB052523

Big Fat Cat

AND THE

SNOW

OF THE

CENTURY

Takahiko Mukoyama

Tetsuo Takashima

with studio ET CETERA

윌북

• 영어를 이해하는 데 굳이 번역문은 필요하지 않다는 저자의 뜻에 따라 우리말 해석을 싣지 않았습니다. 하지만 이 책을 다 본 후에 정확한 번역을 확인하고 싶다면 윌북 영어 카페에 들러주세요. 언제든 환영합니다.
cafe.naver.com/everville □

Miracles come in strange ways.

— words from a fortune cookie

"...78.8, music in the mountains, Spyglass Radio Network..."

"...Hello, all you lonely folks out there listening to the radio on Christmas Day..."

"...Yeah, I know you'd rather be with your family or friends than listening to a DJ on Christmas night — but I'll try my best to keep you from getting lonely."

"There's a huge cold front coming in directly over the Spyglass area. It looks like the weather is going to be really wild tonight. — Heck, this might even be the biggest snowstorm of the century!"

"So shut your garage doors and buy plenty of food. It's going to be a long night."

"Meanwhile, here's a good Christmas number... This one's just for you."

"Oh, darling..."

"Why was I so young...
So young and so hopeful..."

"Why do my memories come back to me..."

"Oooohhh..."

The street corner was a bus stop but someone had stolen all the benches and torn down the roof. The bus stop sign was gone too, so there was no way to know that it was a bus stop. Even the bus drivers sometimes passed it without stopping.

"Thanks for all the nice presents," BeeJees said to Ed, patting the new knitted cap on his head. "You really surprised us."

Ed smiled. He had given presents to almost everyone on Ghost Avenue earlier in the morning.

"You're welcome. Sorry, it was all just cheap stuff."

8

"Naah, good enough for us." BeeJees had noticed the one last present on Ed's lap. "Who's present is that? The cat's?"

Ed took a glance at the red-and-white paper bag on his lap and shook his head.

"No. I already gave the cat a present." Ed pointed at the cat a few feet away. "A whole blueberry pie."

The cat had its head half-buried in a big pie. It noticed and raised its head for a moment, but immediately went back to the pie.

"This one was for Willy," Ed said as he pulled a light pink muffler out of the bag.

"Oh... Yeah," BeeJees nodded.

They sat in silence for a moment.

Snow had covered most of Everville before dawn. The snow fell at a steady pace throughout the morning. Some wind had started to blow, but the weather was reasonably calm. It was still far from a storm.

"Well, don't worry," BeeJees said to Ed. "You already gave Willy a much bigger present."

"Maybe," Ed said, a sad smile on his face.

BeeJees couldn't find anything else to say, so he let his eyes wander off across the street to the old department store on the corner. The building had been closed since the late seventies. The doors were nailed shut, the windows were boarded up, and everything else was broken.

"That store there," BeeJees said abruptly. "It's just a dump now, but you should have seen it when I was a kid. Every Sunday, musicians played on that patio. My dad used to take me to see them when he wasn't drunk. Me and my baby sister each got an ice cream cone from that booth there. They had the best strawberry ice cream ever."

Ed looked at the patio BeeJees was talking about. There were still a few rusty chairs and tables lying around, but it was hard to imagine the patio when it was new. It was just like the rest of Ghost Avenue. A place left behind and forgotten by time.

"Everything seemed to shine in those days." BeeJees sighed, but with a smile still on his face. "But everything ends, sooner or later. Shops close, towns move away... and people... people die. That's just the way it is. There's nothing we can do to stop it."

The snow kept falling without any sound. It fell on both the rich and the poor. It fell on all things old and new. It fell on anything and everything, hiding the world under a soft white cover.

"Sometimes," BeeJees said in a sad but gentle tone. "Sometimes, we just have to let go." ^(놓아주다)

Ed noticed that BeeJees' voice sounded a little bit like Willy's. It brought him some comfort. ^{편안함}

In a peculiar way, Willy had survived, Ed thought. Inside BeeJees. Inside himself. Inside them all. ^{기묘한}

"Some things, we can't change. But some things, we can change. You should know," BeeJees said. "You taught us."

Ed nodded. After a pause, he said to BeeJees. ^{잠깐 멈춤}

"I'm going to the mall on the two o'clock bus. You know, about the shop in the Food Court."

"Good idea," BeeJees said, stretching his arms. "Hope everything goes really great."

"I'm going to decline the offer." ^{거절하다} ^{제안}

"What?"

"I already have a shop here," Ed said. "Besides, they told me I would have to move away from Ghost Avenue if I wanted the shop. Some rule in the health code, they said. And if I rent an apartment, I won't be able to take the cat with me." ^{빌리다}

The cat raised an eyebrow. It seemed to know they were ^{눈썹} talking about it. The empty pie plate from the blueberry pie was ^{접시} lying at the cat's feet.

"Well, it's your life." BeeJees shrugged.

Ed was about to reply when a voice rang out from above them.

"Yo! Everything's ready to go, man!"

It was George. He had appeared on the roof of the old department store holding the end of an electric cable. The other end of the cable was connected to a telephone pole in the street.

Many of the Ghosts heard George's voice. They came out from their usual hiding places into the street. BeeJees stood up and gave George a thumbs-up sign.

"Okay, George. Hit the switch!" BeeJees shouted.

"Gotcha!" George replied. He disappeared behind the edge of the roof. The crowd waited in silence. Ed stood up too, unable to hide his excitement.

Another moment passed in the quiet of the snow, and then suddenly, the roof of the department store lit up with Christmas
(light)
lights. A loud applause rose up from Ghost Avenue. Everybody
박수
yelled "Merry Christmas!"

George started singing a Christmas tune. Within seconds, most of the others joined in, and the street became one big
Christmas choir. BeeJees and Ed smiled at each other.
합창

"It's not anything like the good old days, but it's a lot better than nothing," BeeJees said.

The lights were just cheap toy lights bought at the nearest supermarket, and the electricity was illegally pulled from the
불법으로
telephone pole, but the moment was so wonderful that no one cared. After many long years of silence, Christmas had finally returned to Ghost Avenue.

Standing amid the snow, song, and laughter, BeeJees said
~의 가운데에
once again, softly.

"Yeah. Some things... you can change."

BFC : THE FINAL EPISODE

THE
SNOW
OF THE
CENTURY

"Look, cat," Ed said to the cat once again. The cat just frowned. "I told you. You can't come with me today."

It was ten minutes after two o'clock. The bus had arrived late. Ed had put one foot up on the step of the bus. The cat was just below Ed, looking up at him with an annoyed expression. It was mad because Ed was blocking its rightful path.

"You have to stay here. I'll be back soon."

The cat snarled. It was tired of Ed blocking its way, so it decided to get on the bus.

"Shut the door! Please!" Ed yelled to the bus driver.

"What?" the bus driver replied in a frustrated tone.

The cat was about to jump on the bus.

"Shut the door, now!" Ed repeated.

The driver finally pulled the door lever, grumbling to himself. The door slammed shut just as the cat was getting ready to leap. The cat's eyes widened as it watched the door close. It became angry when it saw Ed standing on the other side of the door.

The cat kept its eyes on Ed as the bus started to drive away. Ed tried to say something to the cat, but the door was too thick. ^{두꺼운}

From inside the bus, Ed watched the cat grow smaller and smaller in the distance as the bus hurried down the street. The cat was still looking at him when the bus rounded a corner several seconds later.

An ^{터무니없는}absurd question suddenly popped into Ed's head.

What if I never see that cat again?

He frowned and ^(shake)shook it off immediately.

Of course I'll see the cat again. Why not?

But all during the bus ride to the New Mall, the image of the cat sitting there alone on the street came back to him again and again and never really disappeared.

The snow was still falling quite lightly when the bus reached the New Mall some twenty minutes later. As the bus crossed the parking lot, Ed could see the empty space where the Pie Festival had been held.

All the tents and rides were already gone and only a few trailers and trucks still remained there. Somehow, it all seemed like one big dream now.

Inside the mall, it was Christmas everywhere. A chorus of Christmas songs greeted Ed, and Christmas lights decorated almost everything in sight. The movie theater near the entrance was showing a romantic comedy featuring a blue snowman.

There were a lot of people in front of the theater waiting for the next showing. A child recognized Ed's face and hollered, "Hey! You're that mustard pie guy!" The child's parents quickly seized him. Ed blushed and walked on. This happened several more times before he reached the Food Court.

A giant Christmas tree was standing in the middle of the Food Court. It was decorated with real cookies and candy from stores in the mall. Zombie Pies was doing an "Evil Santa Pie-Fest."

Ed's feet stopped when he saw the vacant storefront in the Food Court. The steel shutters outside the shop were pulled down.

Ed sat down on a bench in front of the shop. It was the same bench he had sat on a month before. As he looked at the vacant shop, the idea that perhaps everything had been a dream came back to him again.

This can't be real. Maybe I fell asleep on the bench that day, and had a long, long dream. Maybe I'm still on that bench...

For some reason, the thoughts reminded Ed of the paper inside Willy's fortune cookie. He dug into his pocket and found it. It still said the same thing.

Most treasures are in the places you first find them.

Ed raised his head to look at the shop again. Then, he read the words once more.

...in the places you first find them.

It was almost as if Willy was congratulating him. He knew that wasn't possible, but for a moment, Ed actually believed that it might be.

"Ed! Ed Wishbone! I'm so glad you came."

Ed's heart skipped a beat when the owner suddenly patted him on the shoulder. He was so absorbed in his thoughts that he hadn't realized the owner was standing right beside him. Ed quickly folded the fortune paper and slid it back into his pocket.

"Sir. Good afternoon," Ed said, standing up from the bench.

"Did the snow give you any trouble?" The owner asked Ed in his usual joyous tone. "I sure hope not. Now come with me and I'll show you your new shop."

"Uh... sir, I..."

Ed tried to speak, but the owner went straight to the closed shutters. Ed hurried after him, still not sure how to explain.

"Just a second, while I open this shutter here..." the owner said, turning a key in the lock.

"Sir. I'm sorry. I have something to..."

Ed felt his stomach tighten. He imagined what the owner would say when he told him he didn't want the shop. But if he was going to say it, now was his only chance.

"Here we go," the owner said, and threw open the shutters.

The shutters rolled away, revealing an elegant counter with
an open kitchen behind it. The owner turned on the lights and
waved his hand towards the inside of the shop.

"Well?"

Ed was speechless. His eyes were wide open. The owner
noticed this and smiled. He grabbed Ed's arm and pulled him
inside.

"C'mon inside. Take a look."

Ed walked into the shop in a daze.

"Wow..." he whispered. Everything in the shop looked
perfect.

"The last tenant was a pastry shop. They left everything
behind... so you can open your shop at any time," the owner
explained.

Ed nodded, but he wasn't really hearing any of the words.

"Is that the kitchen?" Ed asked.

"It sure is."

"Can I take a look?"

"Of course you can. It's your kitchen."

The owner stepped aside, and Ed moved into the kitchen.
Hidden behind the beautiful glass counter were countless pots
and pans, kitchen utensils, and spice jars. Ed touched the
counter. He stroked its surface softly. It was smooth and spotless.

"This... is all mine?"

"Yes," the owner replied. "All you have to do is sign the
contract."

Ed finally recovered his voice, but now, he wasn't sure what to
say. He took a long deep breath and said to the owner, "I have to
tell you something."

The owner smiled his jolly smile.

"Sure. Anything."

"I..."

I can't accept this prize. I already have a shop.
받아들이다

Ed tried to say, but the words wouldn't come out. The place
of his dreams surrounded him in all its hope and splendor. Ed's
화려함
voice trembled as he finished the sentence.
떨리다

"I... uh... thank you. Thank you for everything."

"My pleasure," the owner said, laughing. "I'm looking
forward to having your pie with lunch everyday."

The owner handed Ed a contract from his coat pocket and
patted him on the shoulder.

"Just sign that and bring it to my office before Wednesday.
See you then."

Ed couldn't help staring at the contract. When he finally
raised his head, the owner was already gone. He was there alone
with the contract.

Ed closed his eyes tight. He hated himself. He realized he
had completely forgotten about Ghost Avenue for the past few
minutes.

"So the little youngster wants Evil Santa, huh?"

Jeremy stood behind the Zombie Pies counter with red and purple makeup on his face, grinning down at a half-scared, half-happy boy who was waiting for his pie.

"Well, Evil Santa wants you too!" Jeremy suddenly raised his voice and a Santa head with a wicked smile popped up from under the counter. The child and his mother both screamed.

So did Ed. Louder.

"AAAGGGHHHH!"

Jeremy was shaken by the scream. He stared at Ed in dumb surprise. Ed had been watching from behind the mother and child. Their eyes met as Ed turned red with embarrassment.

"Oh, it's you," Jeremy said with a sigh. He pulled a rope and the Evil Santa disappeared.

"That was scary," Ed said, slowly recovering from the shock.

"If you think that was scary, go use the men's room. You'll be screaming for the rest of the day."

"Uh... no thank you," Ed said and pointed at the Slime Bucket Pies displayed under the counter glass. "But can I get one of those pies?"

Jeremy frowned but mumbled "Sure," and reached under the counter. He brought out an empty crust shaped like a bowl, and poured a dip of mint slime into the crust. He handed it to Ed with a wooden spoon. Ed took a taste and almost immediately said,

"This is great!"

Jeremy just shrugged.

"This is the best chocolate mint pie I've ever had," Ed repeated.

Jeremy thought Ed was being sarcastic, but Ed really seemed to mean it. *Too bad for Wishbone, he thought, because by the time he opens his shop, Zombie Pies will be gone.*

This was his shop's last week. Jeremy's father had sold the shop to the Everville Rehabilitation Project. But he didn't tell this to Ed.

"You are one strange person," Jeremy mumbled, but not in a bad tone. "Oh, yeah... do you remember my bodyguard?"

"Sure," Ed said rather uneasily. "Of course."

"He was arrested this morning."

"He was?"

"The arrest wasn't a surprise. He did a lot of stuff for my father." Jeremy said the word 'stuff' in a disgusted way. "The real surprise was that the police were able to catch him. He's not an easy man to catch, you know. I think maybe he wanted to get caught."

"Why?" Ed asked.

Jeremy shrugged again. He also knew that if Billy Bob was caught, his father's arrest was not far away, but that was another thing he didn't tell Ed.

"Beats me. I just think so. He didn't like his job very much."
As an afterthought, Jeremy added, "He grew up on Ghost
Avenue, you know."

Ed thought about this for a moment, but couldn't think of
anything to say.

"So when are you going to open?" Jeremy asked, pretending
not to look very interested.

Ed smiled awkwardly for a moment.

"I don't deserve that shop," he said.

Jeremy frowned at Ed while serving another customer a slice
of pie.

Ed said again, "It's too good for me."

"Yeah, yeah. Of course you don't deserve it. Everyone
knows that," Jeremy said. "You only beat me and sixteen other
bakers! Sure, you don't deserve it!"

Ed realized what he was saying and added in a hurry, "Oh,
no no! I didn't mean it that way... Sorry. I'm really proud about
winning the contest! I really am! But that shop... it's just way out
of my league."

"I know, Wishbone, I know."

Jeremy seemed a bit angry, but his voice was calm.

"So I'll tell you what you don't know," Jeremy said as he took the dirty spoon back from Ed. "The only thing worse than getting a chance you don't deserve, is wasting that chance."

Ed fell silent. Jeremy stuck his palm out to Ed. Ed didn't understand why and just stared at Jeremy's palm for a moment.

"$2.55 for the pie," Jeremy said flatly.

"Oh... sorry." Ed fumbled in his pocket and pulled out three dollar-bills in a hurry.

"Thank you very much." Jeremy took the money and reached under the counter for change. "Here's your change," he said and squeezed green slime out from his hand into Ed's palm.

"AAAAAAGHHHHHH!"

This scream was even louder.

The six o'clock bus was the last bus, but Ed decided to take
the five o'clock bus home. This turned out to be a very good
idea, because once the sun set, the snow and wind rapidly grew
stronger. When Ed got off the bus, the snow on the ground was
already up to his ankles. It was only a short walk back to the
theater, but it took him nearly ten minutes to reach the entrance.

*"Reporting live from the New Everville Mall, this is Glen Hamperton
bringing you coverage of the Christmas celebration events scheduled for
tonight."*

The voice from the radio greeted Ed as he closed the door
against the snow. Ed followed the sound of the radio across the
lobby, and into the main theater. George was the first one to
notice Ed's return.

"Yo, Ed. You made it just in time, man. We were getting
kinda worried."

"Sorry," Ed said as he brushed the snow from his head and
shoulders. "The snow's getting worse by the minute."

George, BeeJees, Paddy, Frank, and a few other Ghosts were
huddled around the campfire. Frank was holding his new radio
모이다
in his lap with the volume turned up.

"We were listening to the radio," BeeJees said. "They're
doing live from the mall."

Ed nodded and smiled. Glen Hamperton continued to talk.
She was introducing a local choir group.

George got up and went to the large, steaming pot that sat
김이 나는
beside the campfire. He grabbed a tin cup and dipped it into the
양철
pot.

"C'mon, man. We made you some stew," he said to Ed.
스튜

Ed sat down beside BeeJees and took the cup from George.
Warm, homemade stew with large chunks of vegetables. It was
큰 덩어리
perfect for a day like this.

"So you gave them the bad news?" BeeJees asked as Ed
sipped some stew from the cup.
홀짝거리다

Ed paused for a moment to shake his head.

"I couldn't. I'm planning to go back tomorrow."

BeeJees nodded silently. The radio had started to broadcast a
방송하다
Christmas chorus.

"Cat, cat, cat. Fat, fat, fat," Frank sang along with his own words. He was singing to a poster he had found somewhere.

"You got the roof repaired in time," Ed said to George. He realized that no snow was falling from above. Several wide planks of wood had been laid across the roof, covered with some sort of plastic sheet.

"Yeah. Paddy helped me," George answered proudly, and exchanged a high-five with Paddy.

"Cat fat fat, big fat cat."

Ed couldn't help smiling as he listened to Frank's song. It was so peaceful here. He couldn't believe that it was just a day ago that Willy had passed away. Ed knew that all of them were still sad, but everyone seemed to just go on with their normal life. They had all cried, they had all said good-bye, and now, they all seemed to know that it was time to move on.

It seemed a little strange to Ed, who had thought that after someone you loved died, you were supposed to be sad for a period of time. At least, he had been sad for years, when his mother had passed away. — But he liked the attitude here better. For some reason, it seemed a lot more natural.

Some things we can't change.

Ed took a sip of stew as he looked over at Willy's stroller sitting alone by the wall. It would probably stay there for a long time to come.

Ed had asked the driver of the silent ambulance where he was taking Willy. The driver had answered, "I have no idea." It had all been sad. But sitting there with the Ghosts, in a town that had a very vague sense of time, it didn't feel as sad as it had seemed at first. It was just the way it was.

Ed felt the warmth of the campfire once again. He felt
ashamed [부끄러움을 느끼다] of forgetting, even for a short time, how warm it was
here. The gentle taste of George's stew. The flickering [깜박거림] of the
campfire. Frank's funny song. And the slow, almost frozen sense
of time inside the theater...

Everything he needed was here. He shook his head as he
finished the stew. What was he thinking? He had to be careful.
He had to think real hard because it was...

Ed suddenly stood up in alarm.

His face had become very serious. He looked around the
theater a second time. Finding nothing there, he started towards
the lobby.

"Ed. What's the matter?"

Ed ignored [무시하다] George's question and rushed into the lobby. He
came back only a moment later, much more pale [창백한] than before.

"George," Ed said.

"Where's the cat?"

"Mommy. There was a kitty walking in the snow," the girl said to her mother from the back seat of her family car.

"What did you say, Jane?" her mother asked from the passenger seat in front.

"I saw a kitty-cat walking in the snow," the girl repeated.

"Don't be silly, Jane. Look at how thick the snow is."

"But I know I saw one. It was a big kitty!"

"It was probably just a fire hydrant or something. A cat would freeze to death in this weather."

The girl looked outside again. She knew that her mother was right. But she also knew for sure that she had seen a big fat cat walking along the road. She had even seen the cat's eyes as it looked back at her.

"I just hope kitty's alright," she whispered.

Only the wind answered, with a high shrill cry.

"...*the storm has now entered the Spyglass district and heavy snow
is falling from the sky. The storm is expected to develop into a blizzard
soon...*"

The emergency weather forecast poured out of the radio as
Ed, BeeJees, George, and Paddy gathered in the lobby. Everyone
was covered with snow from head to foot. They looked at each
other without hope.

"BeeJees?" Ed asked.

"Nope. Nowhere," BeeJees answered. "George, did you look
around the junkyard?"

"Yeah. It's already covered with snow. No footsteps."

A heavy silence filled the lobby. Only Frank, who seemed not
to understand the circumstances, kept singing the cat song he had
made up.

"The mall," Ed said. "Maybe he came after me."

Ed checked the only working clock in the theater.

"The last bus is due^{~할 예정인} in about five minutes. I have to go."

George and Paddy looked at each other, then grabbed hold of Ed's arms so he couldn't run off.

"Ed, man! Wait a minute," BeeJees said.

"I have to find the cat! He'll freeze to death in this weather!"

"You'll freeze to death first!" BeeJees shouted. "If you take the last bus to the mall, how are you going to get back? You sure as hell can't walk in this weather!"

Ed wasn't listening. Paddy held Ed tighter, thinking he was going to run towards the door, but Ed was staring at something else.

"Frank," Ed said, blinking^{깜박거리다} his eyes.

"Frank?" BeeJees asked with a puzzled look.

They all followed Ed's eyes to Frank. Frank was still singing his cat song to the poster he held. Ed loosened^{풀다} George and Paddy's grips and walked over to Frank.

"Frank." Ed started to reach for the poster Frank was holding. "Where did you get this?"

"Outside," Frank replied with a smile. "Good man give me."

"Today?" Ed asked again.

"Uh-huh." Frank pointed happily at the poster. "Cat!"

BeeJees and George came beside Ed and took a look at the poster. They held their breath.

"Oh no..." Ed whispered.

Ed grabbed the poster. As soon as he read the first two lines, he headed for the door. George and BeeJees ran after Ed and seized him just as he was about to step outside.

"Let me go! I have to go! He's my cat!"

"Ed!" BeeJees said to him in a desperate tone grabbing him by the collar. The weather outside was really dangerous. BeeJees knew he had to stop him. He shouted in Ed's face, "ED!"

Ed stopped struggling. His face was frozen with fear.

BeeJees spoke as calmly as he could, "Ed. Listen. Do you really think that anyone can catch that cat? I think... maybe the cat knew."

Ed's face grew stern[단호한] as he heard those words.

"I know it sounds crazy! But... but maybe... Maybe the cat knew that you couldn't take him with you. Maybe he left because he wanted you to have that shop in the mall!"

Ed lowered his arms. BeeJees let go. Ed staggered[비틀거리다] back a step, not saying a word.

He had forgotten about the cat.

He was so selfish[이기적인] that he had forgotten all about the cat.

He looked around the lobby at everyone's worried faces, then closed his eyes.

"Damn!" Ed hit his hand hard on the ruins[폐허] of the ticket counter.

"What am I doing? What am I doing!" he shouted.

Full of anger at himself, Ed reached into his pocket, took out the contract from the New Mall, and ripped it into shreds[조각]. He threw the pieces on the floor.

"I'm sorry," Ed said.

And before anybody could move, Ed shoved[떠밀다] George back with both hands and ran through the door.

"Ed!" BeeJees shouted after Ed, but George bumped into him
and they both fell down. When they finally got back to their feet,
Ed had already disappeared into the snow.

George and BeeJees stood at the front door of the theater,
helplessly looking out into the snowstorm. The snow was
no longer a romantic ornament for the streets. It was now a
dangerous enemy.

Behind them, Frank's radio continued to give the weather
forecast in a flat, emotionless tone.

"...the wind has now reached forty miles per hour and it is very
dangerous to walk outside..."

A half hour later, Ed arrived at the New Mall and went straight to the pay phone near the entrance. He found the number of the Everville Health Center on the poster and dialed it. After the tenth ring, a man's voice finally answered. The man seemed tired and reluctant to talk. Ed hurriedly explained what had happened.

"Yes. Big, dark, mean... It's usually walking around Ghost Avenue. Yes! Yes! That's my cat," Ed cried into the phone excitedly. "Have you caught him?"

The passing customers all stared at Ed with suspicious looks on their faces. Ed lowered his voice a little.

"Yes... near Ghost Avenue... Yes... and did you... You chased him for four blocks!?" Ed shouted into the phone. He lowered his voice again after a few middle-aged women pointed at him. "But... but he escaped?"

Half relieved and half disappointed, Ed took a deep breath. The man on the other end seemed outraged.

"Yes... yes. Sir, I'm really sorry the cat ripped your new jacket... yes, and your new pants... and of course, sir, I'll be glad to pay for the belt too, but could you please tell me where you saw him last? Sir? Sir? Please don't hang up!"

But the man hung up. Ed put the phone back down on the hook. He turned from the phone, and almost walked straight into Jeremy, who was standing behind him. Jeremy was dressed to leave work. He had a cell phone in his hand.

"I thought you already went home," Jeremy said, adding in a sarcastic tone, "Or at least something like a home."

Ed stared at Jeremy for a moment. Then he showed him the poster.

"My cat's lost."

Jeremy looked at the poster without much thought. As he read the lines, his frown grew deeper, and finally froze into an expression of horror. He spoke to Ed in a low voice.

"Wishbone. This isn't good news. You could be disqualified for this."

"I don't care."

"Of course you do! This might be your only real chance in life and you..."

Jeremy realized that Ed wasn't looking at him. His eyes were glued to a small crowd that was developing at the center of the mall. The reporter, Glen Hamperton, was in the middle of the crowd with a microphone in one hand. There were also several television cameras moving among the crowd. It was probably the program George and BeeJees had been listening to on the radio.

"Wishbone! Listen to me!"

Jeremy grabbed Ed to make him look his way. Ed did, but his eyes didn't stop on Jeremy's face. They stopped on the cell phone he was holding. An idea had come to his mind.

"Wishbone! I said..."

"I have to borrow this," Ed said, and without waiting for an answer, took the phone from Jeremy's hand. Jeremy opened his mouth wide in annoyance as he watched Ed examine the phone.

"Is this the number for the phone?" Ed asked Jeremy, showing him the phone number taped on the side with cellophane tape.

"Yes. I have so many phones that..."

"Thanks," Ed said and ran off towards the crowd of people.

"Wishbone! Hey, wait a minute! Damn it!"

It took another moment for Jeremy to sigh and run after Ed. By the time Jeremy arrived at the edge of the crowd, Ed was squeezing between people, trying to get to the stage in the middle. Jeremy bit on his lower lip.

"Wishbone... What the hell are you doing?"

Jeremy followed after Ed but was blocked by a group of teenagers who wanted to shake his hand. Jeremy fought them off, but by the time he escaped, Ed had already climbed onto the stage. Guards came forward to stop him, but Glen Hamperton recognized Ed immediately.

"Look who we have here, everyone! The winner of the state pie contest, Ed Wishbone!"

The crowd cheered, thinking Ed was a guest on the show. Ed ignored them and went straight towards Glen.

"Well, what brings you here today, Ed?"

Glen pointed the microphone towards Ed.

"I'm sorry," was all Ed said before he took the microphone from Glen's hand. Glen stared in pure surprise as Ed stepped in front of her to face directly into the camera.

"I'm sorry to interrupt. But this is something very important to me," Ed said, his voice shaking with urgency.

The crowd around the stage heard the serious tone in his voice. The cheering and shouting died down. Ed took a deep breath and held the poster up to the camera.

"My cat is lost in the snow somewhere," he said as the camera focused on the poster. "I need your help. Everyone's help."

In that one moment, the picture of the cat was broadcast to every house in Everville. Snowed-in families sitting in their living rooms watching television all moved closer to the screen to get a better look.

The owner of the New Mall happened to be watching television in his office with a beer in hand. He sprayed his beer all over his desk when he saw the poster.

Jeremy covered his eyes with his right hand and moaned.

On Ghost Avenue, George, Paddy, and BeeJees all crowded around the radio unable to believe what they were hearing. BeeJees dropped his mug on the ground and whispered, "Oh, shit."

"If you have seen this cat, please call me at 555-22xx. This is the cat that ruined the first round of the pie contest yesterday. The health center is chasing him. I didn't know any of this until today. I'm really sorry, and I'm fully responsible for the situation. I'll give back all my prize money and disclaim ownership of the shop in the New Mall as soon as possible."

Ed looked straight into the camera and said to the people of Everville.

"But right now, I have to find my cat. That's all that matters."

A silence followed as Ed stared into the camera for a moment. Nobody in the crowd moved.

After taking a deep breath, Ed gave the microphone back to Glen and stepped off the stage. The crowd remained frozen in position. Ed was sure that everyone was angry at him. He didn't look up.

But after a moment, a woman began clapping her hands. Then a man joined in. A brief pause followed, and then, several other people started clapping their hands. Ed looked around. He was so dumbfounded that he bumped into a bleak-faced Jeremy as he stepped out of the crowd.

"What the hell was that?" Jeremy asked in an angry voice.

"I need to borrow your phone for a while," Ed said.

"Forget the phone, you idiot! Do you know what you've done? You just threw away the best chance of your life!"

Ed gave him one short nod and headed down the aisle.
Jeremy followed along, shouting at him.

"What stupid reason was that for? The cat doesn't even have
a collar! Anybody would have thought it was a stray! Why did
you have to say on TV that it was your cat?"

Ed didn't slow down for a second. He was headed straight
outside. Jeremy sighed, shook his head, and with a slight change
of tone in his voice, continued shouting at Ed.

"And what are you going to do without a car? Walk!? It's
nine degrees below zero outside, you nitwit!"

Ed finally came to a stop by the exit. The snow had become
even fiercer in the last few minutes. The weather outside was so
violent that even Ed, despite his determination, had to stop for a
moment.

"You're really going to choose a cat over a shop in the mall?" Jeremy asked Ed one last time.

"The cat... he chose me," Ed replied.

"You're so damn stupid, it's almost illegal," Jeremy said, as he pulled out his car keys and headed for the door. "You wait here."

When Jeremy opened the door, the snowstorm noticed, and attacked full force. Jeremy winced, but stood his ground. The last thing he did before stepping out into the snow was to say to Ed,

"And you better check on that 'he' part."

Ed watched in surprise, as Jeremy dashed through the snow to his car. He wanted to thank him, but he had no time to do that now.

The snowstorm had arrived.

"Okay folks, I have a message here from one of our listeners."

"Hello, SRN. I'm a college student visiting my grandparents in Everville for winter vacation. It's been a great Christmas for me. All the family together, delicious homemade dinners, watching a lot of old movies, a warm fireplace, and a whole bunch of presents!"

"I have to tell you... Christmas is the best time of year."

Jeremy's black limousine fought through the snow, swerving and sliding, as they drove south on Valley Mills Drive. The car routinely skidded sideways off the road, flinging Ed across the back seat countless times. He sat up quickly but was soon flung again, and each time he banged his head into something hard.

"Please keep the car steady!"

Ed cried to Jeremy from the back seat after a fifth encounter with the back door. Jeremy, driving with almost zero visibility, shouted back angrily.

"It would help if you closed the damn window! We're going to catch pneumonia!"

Snow was blowing in through the back window. Driving the limousine was even more difficult with snow swirling not only outside, but inside the car too.

Ed kept his eyes on the roadside with his head poking halfway out the window. But it was impossible to spot a single cat in this snow. Ed's lips had gone from blue to black, and he could barely keep his eyes open in the cold wind. Hope ran out of him with every passing second.

Jeremy took a glance at Ed and saw the desperate look on his face. He swallowed once.

"Look, I don't want to sound cruel, but I'm sure you've realized by now that if the cat were still outside, it would already be dead."

Jeremy took another look in the rearview mirror. Ed seemed not to have heard what Jeremy had said.

"Wishbone! Are you listening, dammit? We could easily die out here too, you know!"

Ed bit on his lower lip. The big roadside sign for the New Mall stood on the other side of the road. Everything beneath it was already buried in the snow. He knew Jeremy was right. They could have passed the cat anywhere. His mind told him it was pointless.

But the image of the cat sitting there on the street earlier today, and the image of that same cat lying beneath cold snow, slowly freezing to death, wouldn't allow Ed to give up.

Some things you can change.

He had to believe. He was so damn tired of losing everything.

Jeremy's cell phone suddenly rang. Ed fumbled for the phone. It took him a moment to press the talk button with his cold fingers. It was a short but horrible moment for Ed. He was scared that the caller might hang up.

"It's probably just another crank call," Jeremy muttered.

"Hello?" Ed said into the phone. "Hello?"

There was some background noise, but no voice at the other end. It seemed like another hoax. There had been five of them already. But this time, after a long pause, a small girl's voice came from the speaker.

"I saw your kitty," the girl said. "It was walking down Valley Mills Drive. Near the big sign for the mall."

"Valley Mills Drive? Here!?" Ed repeated. They had just passed that 'big sign' moments ago. "Could you tell me when...?"

But the phone was already dead. The child had hung up, perhaps she was too shy or scared to talk anymore.

"Thank you," Ed said softly into the phone and rushed to the window once again. He said to Jeremy, "A girl called. She said she saw my cat somewhere near here!"

"And of course you believe her," Jeremy said in a sarcastic tone.

Ed went back and forth across the car trying to spot something — any sign of the cat. Jeremy opened his window too. The snow flew through the car now, making the inside of the car almost the same as the outside. They looked and looked, but all they could see was white land.

Ed spotted the sign for the sandwich shop he had stopped at. He could almost see a phantom image of himself and the cat on the roadside, still looking for a new job.

Everything that had happened since then — both the good
and the bad — the cat had always been there with him. The
image of the cat lying dead in the snow rose up in his mind
again, and he closed his eyes to fight the tears.

"Willy..." Ed said, almost like a prayer. It was the only word
he knew that seemed stronger than the despair outside. And that
very name brought something back into his mind.

The fortune paper.

Something told him to take the paper out of his pocket and
read it one final time. So he did that.

Most treasures are in the places you first find them.

And this time, the words made perfect sense. Ed jumped to the window again and stuck his head out as far as he could. The snow attacked him fiercely, but about a hundred feet ahead, he was able to see the road fork towards Old Everville — towards the Outside Mall.

It wasn't about the shop, Ed thought. *It never was.*

"Turn left at the next corner!" Ed said to Jeremy.

"What!?" Jeremy thought he'd heard wrong.

The road to the left at the traffic signal was very narrow and was already deeply covered in snow. It wasn't even a road anymore. It was just a pile of snow.

"I need to get to the Outside Mall. Turn left at that corner. It's over the hill."

"That corner?" Jeremy shouted, pointing at the nonexistent road ahead. "*That corner!?* You're insane! We'll get stranded and die!"

Ed took a deep breath and calmly said,

"Then let me out at the corner."

"You're kidding."

"I'm not. Pull over by the side and I'll get off."

The corner was approaching fast. A precious moment passed before Jeremy was able to say anything.

"Now, wait a minute. Let's consider this again. You want me to drive this extra fancy limo into that pool of snow?!"

The corner was now moments away. Jeremy caught a glimpse of Ed getting ready to go out into the snow and spoke faster.

"Do you know what this car cost?! The front bumper probably cost more than everything in your bank account! And look! This new audio system cost something like... damn! TO HELL WITH IT! I'M RICH ANYWAY!"

Jeremy yanked the steering wheel to the left and the car spun off towards Old Everville, crashing head first into the heavy drift.

"And now the road down to Standpoint is completely cut off. All public transportation in the Spyglass area has been halted. Please remain indoors until further notice..."

Frank's radio kept repeating the same message over and over. BeeJees, George, and Paddy all sat around the fire, looking glumly at the radio. The wind shook the old theater to its foundations, reminding them how dangerous it was outside.

BeeJees sighed.

"There's no way the cat could still be alive."

No one answered. George and Paddy tended the fire in sad silence. BeeJees stared at the floor.

"Uh-uh," someone said.

BeeJees raised his eyes and looked at George and Paddy, but both shook their heads. It wasn't either of them. The voice had come from behind BeeJees.

"Uh-uh," Frank said again, smiling his toothless smile. He
was rolling around in his wagon.

"What, Frank?" BeeJees said, a little annoyed. ^{귀찮은 듯이}

Frank gave them all a big proud smile and said,

"Eddie findie cat."

They all stared at each other. Frank nodded to himself as if
he were sure. Then he looked at Willy's stroller and nodded a
second time. With a great big smile, he pointed straight towards
Old Everville and repeated in a confident voice. ^{자신 있는}

"Ed always findie cat."

    The car had run off the road near the top of the hill. It
landed in a ditch, one tire buried deep in the snow. The engine
was still alive, but the headlights were both smashed.

    Ed opened the back door of the limousine and stepped
out into the snow. He had hit his head. His right temple was
bleeding a little.

    He peered inside the car to check if Jeremy was okay. Jeremy
seemed to be shaken-up, but he wasn't injured. Ed sighed with
relief, but before Jeremy could recover enough to stop him, he
started walking down the hill, straight into the snowstorm.

The snow came up to his 무릎 knees, and it was difficult to walk even a few steps. The wind 위협하다 threatened his balance and the blowing snow 숨막히게 하다 suffocated him. But he didn't stop. He 간신히 걷다 waded forward, digging through the snow, fighting his way down the hill.

His whole body was so cold. His feet seemed like someone else's feet.

Down below, he could see nothing but white, white, white land. Snow had covered everything. He remembered that the Outside Mall was at the bottom of the hill, but all he could see was snow. Even if the cat were somewhere down there, he had no idea how to find it. But he kept going anyway.

Halfway down the hill, his legs gave out ^(힘이 다하다) and he fell forward, ^{굴러 떨어지다}tumbling down the hill, creating a long cloud of snow in the air. He rolled all the way down, and finally stopped after sliding another few feet across flat ground. He ^{신음하다}moaned in pain but got up.

"Caaat!" Ed shouted into the blizzard, but the wind ^{지우다}erased his voice. He called out even louder, "Caaat! Where are you!? Caaaat!!"

Only the wind answered. Ed was too cold and too tired to think.

The snow was all around him. It came from all directions, completely blinding him. His hands were half-frozen and the cold had entered his lungs. He was losing his sense of direction. He knew he was somewhere near the shop, but everything was hidden under the snow. The world was just one big white blur.

"Cat..." Ed didn't know if he was standing or not. He realized he had closed his eyes sometime before. He was so tired.

"Cat... I'm sorry..."

Then, everything began to fade.

Everything became white with the snow.

Willy?

"Son, you're going to freeze to death if you sleep here,"
Willy said with a smile. Ed got to his knees, thinking vaguely,
you should put on this muffler, Willy. It's really cold today.

"Willy," Ed said. "I'm sorry. I... I was late again. I'm always
late."

Willy smiled.

"No, Ed."

Despite all the wind and snow, Willy's voice was clear and
calm. It still had that warm tone.

"You were never late. You've always made it just in time.
You found that cat just before it starved to death. You learned a
great lesson just before you gave up. You found the real meaning
of winning just before you won... And you saved my soul... all,
just in time."

Ed shook his head.

"No. I... I... Willy... I've lost my cat... I went after him, but I was late again. He saved me. He was always there with me and I was late..."

Willy just stood there smiling.

"No, Ed. I told you. You were always there in time. You just didn't see it that way."

"But Willy... I... I..."

The moon somehow appeared in the sky through the snow. It was the same moon as the one they had seen on the way to the hospital. It was still beautiful. Willy smiled one final time.

"You've always made it in time... and you made it just in time again," said Willy. "Now wake up."

"Willy...?"

Ed opened his eyes halfway and realized he had fainted ^{기절하다}
somewhere in the snow. He was barely able to get to his knees.
He looked around for Willy, but there was nothing but the
snowstorm around him.

"Willy... I..."

Ed stopped, noticing that he was holding something in his
right hand beneath the snow. He pulled his hand out and a string ^끈
came out from under the snow. He didn't realize what it was for
a moment. He just stared at it.

But slowly, very slowly, he realized that he had seen the string
before. He pulled the string from under the snow. A ragged ^{해진}
gingerbread man was connected to it.

Ed opened his eyes wider and pulled on the string frantically. ^{미친 듯이}
A line of gingerbread man decorations popped out of the snow
in front of him. It was a decoration from Pie Heaven's front
window.

Ed got to his feet. The storm seemed to have weakened a
little. Ed quickly tugged on the line. The other end was stuck ^{당기다}
under a snow-covered box a few feet away.

Ed rushed over to the box and wiped the snow off the top of the box. It was his old glass showcase.

Ed used his hands to find the edge of the case. This was the showcase he had always stored his blueberry pies in. He pulled off the top of the case and looked inside. The snow had penetrated the case, filling up half of its interior. Ed dug the snow out with both hands, ignoring the pain in his fingertips. He finally managed to get most of the snow out.

"No..." Ed gasped.

Buried under the snow, in a corner of the case, was a ball of fur.

"Oh no..."

The ball of fur didn't move. Ed knelt down on the snow with trembling hands.

"Cat..." Ed said. The tears he had held back came now. He said in a weak voice, "Cat... wake up... please."

Ed reached out and touched the body of the cat. It was cold.
Ed gulped. A shiver ran down his spine.

"Cat... come on. I found you. I found you again. This time,
I know I'm not late. Now wake up!"

From the day it had come into Pie Heaven, it had always
been his cat. It had preferred his blueberry pies right from the
start. It was his one and only cat.

"You can't sleep here, cat! C'mon, I wasn't late, damn it! I
swear I wasn't late this time!"

There was no answer. The cat lay perfectly still. But somehow,
Ed knew the cat could hear him. The cat had always come back
to him, and it would come back, one final time.

"C'mon! I'll bake you all the blueberry pies you want. Just...
just wake up. Please. CAT! WAKE UP!"

But still, no response. No response at all. All strength began
to run out of Ed. He stood there a while staring at the motionless
body of the cat. It seemed so cold lying there in the snow.

Ed took off his muffler and covered the cat. He bent down [구부리다]
and picked the cat up, wrapping it inside the muffler. The cat's
body was still slightly [약간] warm. And heavy. He realized this was the
first time he had ever held the cat and it made him cry.

"I'm sorry... I forgot... for a moment there in the mall, I
forgot... and you... you probably thought I... I'm sorry, cat."

The cat moved. Ed thought he had imagined it, but the cat
slowly looked up at him with a big frown.

"Cat?"

The cat was looking around for blueberry pie and found
none. In a very frustrated mood, it glared at Ed for waking it up
during a perfectly good nap [낮잠]. It sneezed [재채기하다] once and swiftly [재빠르게] jumped
out of Ed's hands.

Ed was completely frozen for a moment. He stared at the
cat with disbelief [불신]. The cat was taking a stretch as if nothing had
happened.

"Cat...? You're... okay?"

The cat yawned [하품하다]. Ed reached out for the cat, but the cat, as
always, scratched him.

"You're okay?!" Ed said. "Oh my God. You're okay!"

Ed closed his eyes tightly [꽉] as great relief rushed through him.
It was a moment so unbelievable [믿을 수 없는] that he couldn't even breathe
for a few seconds. He opened his eyes again and looked at the
cat. The cat was still staring at him.

"I come all this way to find you, and you're taking a nap, you
damn thing," Ed said with a smile on his face, tears in his eyes
and snow in his hair.

As Ed wiped his eyes, he realized that the snow and wind were beginning to calm down. Only a gentle shower of snowflakes was now falling from the sky.

"Cat... all during the time I was searching for you, I was thinking why I needed you so much. And I think I finally know now," Ed said as he knelt down in front of the cat. A beautiful white world enveloped them as they sat there together in the ruins of Pie Heaven.

"Mom gave me the recipe, Willy gave me the courage... but you..." Ed paused.

"You gave me the reason. Even when nobody came to my shop, you were always there to eat my pies. You were the one that made me a baker. I would have quit baking a long time ago if it wasn't for you." Ed smiled and said to the cat in a voice that was his most sincere, "Thanks. Thanks a lot."

For a moment, time itself seemed to pause. The world was quiet and forgiving <small>용서하다</small> in the silent snowfall. Even then <small>(그때조차도)</small>, Ed knew in the back of his mind, that time would start moving again soon. He would have to apologize to a lot of people, and he would also have to find a way to build a new life. But for now, he didn't care. It was only him and the cat — just as it was in the beginning.

Ed stood up.

You are a baker, Ed. Just a baker without a shop. Now go back. Bake your pie.

"I will, Willy," Ed whispered to himself as he wrapped the muffler around him. The cat had become tired of waiting. It decided to scratch Ed again.

"I know, I know. I'll bake you a blueberry pie as soon as we get home. I have to get the Magic Pie Shop ready anyway."

The cat scratched him for an answer. Ed smiled.

"And cat, you really need a name," he said.

The snowstorm had reduced[감소시키다] all the colors in the world to a big white land of snow. In the distance, a police siren was coming their way. Ed and the cat started walking back towards town, their footsteps lined close together in the snow.

This night will end, but soon, a new day will begin in the town of Everville.

There are a lot of pies in this world.

Some are sweeter than others.

Some are sour.

Some are even spicy or bitter or hot.

But that's not important.
What's important is that every pie is different.
Every pie has its own taste.

My pie may not be sweet — it may seem funny at first sight. But it's all I have, and it's all mine.

And whatever the pie... whatever the taste... if you have friends, family, and of course... a cat you love... that pie will always taste good.

Even if it is... a mustard pie.

The End

BFC Presents :

Short Story Collection

Moochies 86

Look & See 88

The Last Pages of the Red Book 90

A Good Man Is Hard to Find 96

Short Story Collection에 관한 **One Point**

● Look & See

Look & See에 나와 있는 구절들은 제목부터 연결해서 읽어보면 구성된 장소의 부록('접착제+사물'형식)으로 이어진 하나의 긴 문장이 됩니다. 이런 식으로 끝없이 이야기를 이어나갈 수 있습니다. 영어는 뒤에 부록만 붙이면 얼마든지 문장을 만들 수 있는 언어라는 사실을 보여주는 예입니다. 조금 과장된 예를 들어보았는데 그 재미를 한번 느껴보세요.

● The Last Pages of the Red Book

Red Book의 희생자에게는 Father Gibbons도 모르는 숨겨진 공통점이 하나 있다는 사실······.

● A Good Man Is Hard to Find

A Good Man Is Hard to Find는 Flannery O'Connor가 쓴 단편소설의 제목이기도 합니다. 헨리의 모험을 다 읽고 난 후 다시 Big Fat Cat 시리즈를 읽어보시길 바랍니다. 자세히 들여다보면 여기저기 헨리의 모습이 보일지도······.

LOOK & SEE ...

...THROUGH THE WINDOW...

...OF AN AIRPLANE...

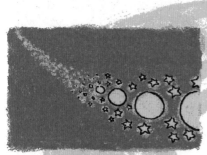

...ACROSS THE GALAXY...

...ALONG THE STARS...

...AROUND THE PLANET...

...ON A STICK...

...IN A PARK...

...INSIDE A DOME...

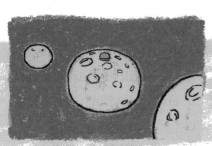

...WITH OTHER MOONS...

...ON THE MOON...

...IN MY ROOM...

...THROUGH THE WINDOW...

...OF AN AIRPLANE...

THE
LAST PAGES
OF THE
RED BOOK

F ather Patrick Gibbons had searched for the Red Book his whole life. His father had been killed with an axe [도끼] when he was still a small child, and his mother had been arrested [체포되다] for his father's murder. But little Patrick knew his mother was innocent [무죄의], because he had seen it — the scene of his father's death.

His father had brought home an old red book that afternoon, and had been reading it late into the night. When Patrick said

90

good night to his father, his father didn't seem to hear him. His father's eyes were glued^{고정된} to the pages of the book. They looked like the eyes of a dead man. Dark, cold eyes just staring into the book.

Hours after going to bed, Patrick could not sleep. He could not forget his father's dark eyes. Finally, he climbed quietly out of bed and walked down the hall to the living room.

Just as Patrick peeked through the keyhole in the living room door, his father turned the last page of the Red Book. What happened next determined^{결정하다} the rest of Patrick's life.

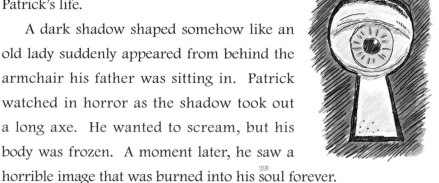

A dark shadow shaped somehow like an old lady suddenly appeared from behind the armchair his father was sitting in. Patrick watched in horror as the shadow took out a long axe. He wanted to scream, but his body was frozen. A moment later, he saw a horrible image that was burned into his soul^{영혼} forever.

He would never forget the heavy sound of the axe.

The next thing he knew, it was morning. He was lying in a police station. A police officer told him that his mother had a 'fight' with his father, and that Patrick was going to be put in an orphanage.^{고아원}

He tried to explain what he saw through the keyhole, but no one believed him. They never found any 'Red Book' at the scene of the crime.^{범죄} He tried harder and harder to explain, and

eventually, they put him in a mental hospital. He stayed there
for two long years.

He learned there, that no one would ever believe his story,
and that his parents would never come back.

After he was released from the hospital, Patrick went to a
Christian school and became a priest, but he never for one day
forgot about the evil Red Book.

Years passed, and Patrick became a respected priest at the
Everville Memorial Church. He was finally beginning to think
that maybe it had all been in his imagination. That perhaps his
mother really had killed his father. That he had just imagined
the shadow with the axe, because he didn't want to believe what
he had really seen.

After all, that was what the doctors had said.

Then one day a member of the church, Jonathan Peters, was
killed in his living room while reading a book.

He had been killed with an axe.

Everything was the same. The man's wife was arrested for

murder.

Patrick knew the Peters well. He knew the couple loved each other very much. He knew that she did not kill him.

The Peters had a five-year old boy. His name was Eric. Patrick had been his teacher in Sunday school last year. So when he heard the news, he rushed over to the Peters's house.

The police were everywhere. Patrick found Eric lying on the couch. He seemed not to understand what was happening.

"Eric. It's me. Father Gibbons. You have to listen to me. This is very important," Patrick said to Eric.

Eric's eyes were distant, but he nodded.

"Did you see someone with an axe?"

Eric shook his head.

"Did your father have a red book with him last night?"

Eric nodded. Patrick held his breath.

"Where is it now?" he whispered, not wanting the police to hear.

"My room. I found it before I saw daddy..."

"Wait here."

Patrick headed down the hall, making the sign of the cross.

The police were still busy in the living room. No one seemed to have searched Eric's room yet. The room was dark, but the Red Book glowed on Eric's bed. It was the same book he had seen in his father's hands so

long before.

"I've finally found you, demon." Patrick whispered and took out a lighter from his pocket. "Now you can go back to hell."

Patrick picked the book up and was about to set it on fire, when he suddenly felt an incredible urge to look inside.

What was it that killed my father?

What could possibly be written in the book of the devil?

He had to know. He had wondered all those years what his father had been reading when he was killed. What had made his father's eyes so dark... and so... so satisfied.

Holding the lighter in one hand, Patrick slowly opened the book. The book instantly opened to the last page.

It said:

Here's what your father saw, Patrick.

"No."

Patrick barely spoke the word before an axe was buried in his back. He fell to the ground, spitting blood from his mouth. He tried desperately to use the lighter, but he had dropped the book on the floor and it had rolled away. The Red Book landed right in front of Eric, who had been standing in the doorway unnoticed. Eric reached down for the book.

"Eric, don't..." Patrick said, his mouth full of blood. But it was too late. Eric had opened the book.

"NO!" Patrick shouted, but nothing happened. Eric flipped a few pages, leaned his head to one side, and then brought the book to Patrick.

(페이지를) 넘기다

"I can't read yet," he said.

Patrick thought he heard the agonized cry of the demon as he smiled for the last time in his life. Then, he brought the lighter to the book. The book burst into flames.

고통스러운

Father Patrick Gibbons died then, watching the last pages of the book burn to ashes in front of him.

재

No one has seen the Red Book ever since.

THE END

A GOOD MAN IS HARD TO FIND

1. Henry Goodman Isn't a Good Man

This is the small town of Everville. It's a middle-class town located on a mountainside. Roughly, eight thousand people live here, work here, study here, and sleep here. Henry Goodman is one of them. His name is Goodman, but he isn't really a good man.

For one thing, he's always been irresponsible. He used to have a wife and a daughter, and a nice place he called home. But Henry liked to gamble. And he gambled a lot. He spent most of his income at a small racetrack in Glassview. He didn't really care if he won or lost. He just liked the excitement.

But his wife cared. And she cared very much.

So one day, his wife took their daughter and left the house. Henry received a letter in the mail a week later, telling him he would never see them again. Henry didn't blame his wife. He'd known it would eventually happen, and he was just glad it was over.

In the days that followed, Henry just woke up, went to work, came home, slept, and went to work again. Sometimes he ate lunch, and sometimes he ate dinner, but rarely both, and never breakfast. He continued to go to the racetrack once or twice a week, sometimes closing his shop at noon.

2. Henry Goodman Forgets Something Important

Henry's shop was located in the Outside Mall, a worn-out, forgotten shopping center in Old Everville. The only other shop still open at the mall (except for the cafeteria) was some kind of pie or cake shop (he didn't know which, and he didn't care) that some young kid from the city had opened. Heaven-something. Good name, because the mall really needed help from up there.

Several months ago, some guy came to Henry's shop to give him an eviction notice. The guy said the mall was going to be torn down by that millionaire in town. The guy also gave Henry another notice to give to the kid next door, but Henry forgot, and after a few weeks, he lost the piece of paper.

At first, he worried about his shop. But after a month of nothing happening, Henry decided it had probably been a mistake, and that everything was going to be okay. So he kept gambling until he lost his house. Even then, Henry wasn't too worried, because he still had his shop, and he could live there. He gambled away what little money he still had.

3. Henry Goodman Loses His Shop

One day, after a morning at the shop that was slow as usual, Henry closed the shop and went to the racetrack. He had an unusually lucky day and won over fifty dollars. He thought his 운 luck was finally changing.

휘파람을 불다
Whistling a tune, Henry went back to the Outside Mall happy 만족스러운 and content, until he saw his shop being torn down.

Henry stood there at the bus stop for some time. He spotted the shocked city kid sitting in the 잔해 ruins of his shop. He suddenly remembered that he had forgotten to give the kid the eviction notice. Henry got scared and ran away.

Henry went to a motel on the 교외 outskirts of town to sleep for the night. Unfortunately, the only room available was a family room. Henry rented the room, using up almost all of the money he had won at the racetrack. He realized that he only had five dollars left when he lay down on the bed.

That evening, lying alone in a room with two empty beds, he remembered his wife and daughter, and for the first time, he really understood that he was never, ever going to see them again. It wasn't a joke. Life wasn't a joke. The cold, quiet motel room seemed more real than anything he had ever felt.

He got up and ran away from the motel.

4. Henry Goodman Gets a New Job

Henry took the bus to the New Mall. He didn't have anything else to do. He bought a slice of pizza and ate it while sitting on a bench. It was warm in the mall, and the bench felt good.

Why not just sleep here?

Henry thought this was a good idea until some janitors found him and kicked him out of the mall.

Discouraged, Henry sat down at the front entrance of the mall. Sometime near an hour later, a middle-aged man came running out.

"Did you see someone with a bandage on his head?" the man asked him.

Henry shook his head. The man looked at him suspiciously and asked, "I'm sorry, but why are you sitting here?"

Henry had nothing to lose, so he told the man everything. The man, who turned out to be the owner of the New Mall, was very interested to hear that Henry had been a shop-keeper at the late Outside Mall.

"Maybe this isn't just a coincidence," the owner said. "I think I have good reason to help you."

Henry didn't know what that good reason might be, but he was really grateful when the owner offered him a job as a night maintenance man at the New Mall.

He took the job.

5. Henry Goodman Tries

On that day, something changed inside Henry. A very simple but important dream took hold of him: He wanted to see his wife and daughter just one more time and apologize to them. But before he could do that, he had to prove, to himself, that he could be a better man.

So his days at the racetrack became less and less frequent, and he worked more and more. The job wasn't bad, and the owner was a nice man. For some reason, the owner seemed to trust him, and sometimes he even ran small personal errands for the owner, such as going to Ghost Avenue to buy pies.

He had no idea why the owner wanted pies from a shop in the ghetto. But he did it anyway.

There was one strange thing, though.

Henry had vaguely recognized the man selling the pies. After thinking carefully, he decided it was probably just his imagination.

6. Henry Goodman and the State Pie Festival

All went well until the State Pie Festival.

A week before the festival, the owner had suddenly assigned Henry as the security chief of the festival grounds. He felt incredibly honored by the assignment, but he was also a little scared. Nevertheless, Henry tried his best.

Guarding the Zombie Pies parade was the toughest part of the job, but he remembered his daughter had loved that shop, so he was proud to do it.

It was almost the end of the Pie Contest, when it happened. He had been guarding the judges' booth when he saw someone that looked like his wife and daughter walk past him. He rubbed his eyes. It wasn't an illusion. His daughter had grown, but it was her.

He followed after them without thinking much.

Once outside the main tent, his wife turned around and their eyes met. They both froze, but his daughter immediately ran towards him. She cried out, "Daddy!"

He would never forget the moment he hugged his daughter

for the first time in years. She had gotten so much bigger.

His wife watched in silence as Henry listened to his daughter talk about Zombie Pies. Something about Henry's patience made her say to him,

"Henry, we moved back to Old Everville last week. There's a room in our house that's empty. If you want to be in our family again, we'll be waiting at the bus stop."

He heard his wife's words but he doubted his ears. It was too good to be true. And in a moment of panic, Henry got confused. He wanted to live with them more than anything, but he also thought that he might ruin everything again. So he did the stupidest thing in his life. He ran away.

He knew he would regret it for the rest of his life, but he couldn't stop himself. He ran back to the main tent.

7. Henry Goodman Does It Again

He was sobbing when he got back to the judges' booth. He
had just ruined his only chance at happiness. He was so sad, he
was sure that this was the lowest point of his life. He was wrong.

Henry glanced inside the judges'
booth.

The booth was a complete mess.
Someone had destroyed every pie in
the booth. The staff and audience
were in a huge riot. And it was all
his fault. He had left his guard.

Henry saw the crowd shouting
at the owner. He had never been
more scared in his life. So he did what he had done all his life.

He ran away.

He ran through the crowd, through the festival grounds, and
straight through the main gate. He kept running until he was
completely out of breath.

8. Way to Go, Henry Goodman!

He finally stopped near the road, feeling terrible and sick of
himself. He had done it again. He had disappointed everyone
again. He felt that he was the most useless fool in the history of the
world.

"Henry, you came," a voice said to him.

Henry looked up and found his wife and daughter standing in front of him.

"I knew you'd come!" His daughter put both arms around him.

Henry stood there bug-eyed. He looked around and saw that he was standing at the bus stop near the mall.

"Here comes the bus," his daughter said, pointing down the road.

His wife told him, "I think you've changed a lot, and I think you deserve a second chance."

Henry still couldn't say anything, but he nodded. The bus arrived and they got on it together. Behind them, the speakers were announcing the rematch at the pie contest, but Henry was so busy hugging his daughter that he didn't hear anything.

Henry Goodman isn't really a good man. But he isn't a bad man either. He doesn't always get the best pie, but still, there are a lot of pies in this world.

A GOOD MAN IS HARD TO FIND

The End ☺

BIG FAT CAT'S
3 COLOR
DICTI🐱NARY

BIG FAT CAT
and the
SNOW OF THE CENTURY

빅팻캣의 3색사전

~빅팻캣과 100년 만의 폭설 편~

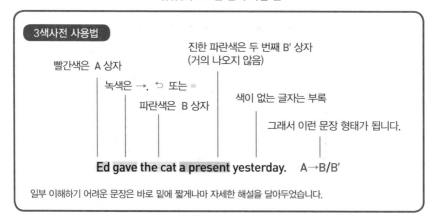

3색사전 사용법

빨간색은 A 상자

진한 파란색은 두 번째 B' 상자
(거의 나오지 않음)

녹색은 →, ↩ 또는 =

파란색은 B 상자

색이 없는 글자는 부록

그래서 이런 문장 형태가 됩니다.

Ed gave the cat a present yesterday.   A→B/B'

일부 이해하기 어려운 문장은 바로 밑에 짧게나마 자세한 해설을 달아두었습니다.

3색사전은 스토리 부분의 영문을 색깔로 구분하여 문형을 한눈에 알아볼 수 있도록 만든 힌트북입니다.
물론 '정답'은 아닙니다. 영문을 이해하기 위한 하나의 길잡이로 이용해주시기 바랍니다.

"...78.8, music in the mountains, Spyglass Radio Network..."   불완전한 문장   p.5

본문의 5쪽부터 8쪽 첫째 줄까지는 모두 Spyglass Radio Network(스파이글래스 지역의 라디오 방송국)의 크리스마스 특집방송에서 흘러나온 내용이에요.

"...Hello, all you lonely folks out there listening to the radio on Christmas Day..."   불완전한 문장

라디오 방송의 DJ가 들려주는 말들입니다. you=lonely folks이며, 남은 부분은 모두 lonely folks를 꾸며주는 화장품과 화장문이에요.

"...Yeah, I know you'd rather be with your family or friends than listening to a DJ on Christmas night — but I'll try my best to keep you from getting lonely."   A→B but A→B   p.6

우리나라에서는 크리스마스라면 낭만적인 이벤트를 연상하지만, 미국에서는 가족과 함께 보내는 소중한 날이라는 이미지가 강합니다. 우리나라의 '설날'과 비슷한 느낌이라고 할까요.

"There's a huge cold front coming in directly over the Spyglass area.   A=B

It looks like the weather is going to be really wild tonight.   A=B

— Heck, this might even be the biggest snowstorm of the century!"
A=B

"So shut your garage doors and buy plenty of food.   (A)→B and (A)→B

It's going to be a long night."   A=B

"Meanwhilwe, here's a good Christmas number... This one's just for you."
A=B... A=B

number에는 '숫자'란 의미 외에 음악의 '곡'이라는 의미도 있습니다. 여기서는 '크리스마스용 곡'이란 의미로 쓰였어요. 뒷부분의 one은 Christmas number의 대역이에요.

"Oh, darling..."   불완전한 문장   p.7

"Why was I so young...   A=B

So young and so hopeful..."　　불완전한 문장

"Why do my memories come back to me..."　　A↺

"Oooohhh..."　　불완전한 문장

"On Christmas Daaay..."　　불완전한 문장

The street corner was a bus stop but someone had stolen all the benches
　　and torn down the roof.　　A=B but A→B and (A)→B

The bus stop sign was gone too, so there was no way to know that it was a
　　bus stop.　　A=B, so A=B

Even the bus drivers sometimes passed it without stopping.　　A→B
　　it은 앞 문장에 나오는 bus stop의 대역입니다.

"Thanks for all the nice presents," BeeJees said to Ed, patting the new
　　knitted cap on his head.　　A→B

"You really surprised us."　　A→B

Ed smiled.　　A↺

He had given presents to almost everyone on Ghost Avenue earlier in the
　　morning.　　A→B

"You're welcome.　　A=B

　　Sorry, it was all just cheap stuff."　　A=B

"Naah, good enough for us."　　불완전한 문장
　　Naah는 no와 같은 의미지만 조금 수줍어하는 이미지가 있어요. good enough는 본래
　　It was good enough로, '(우리에겐) 아주 충분하다'는 뜻입니다.

BeeJees had noticed the one last present on Ed's lap.　　A→B
　　영어에서 '무릎'을 의미하는 단어는 두 종류로 구분됩니다. lap은 앉은 자세에서 허리부

터 무릎까지의 부분이고, knee는 구부려지는 관절의 앞부분을 가리켜요.

"Who's present is that?   A=B

Who's는 Who is를 줄여서 쓴 형태가 아니라 Ed's, George's에서 쓰이는 's와 같은 의미입니다.

The cat's?"   불완전한 문장

Ed took a glance at the red-and-white paper bag on his lap and **shook his head.**   A→B and (A)→B

"No. I already **gave the cat a present.**"   불완전한 문장   A→B/B'

Ed pointed at the cat a few feet away.   A→B

"A whole blueberry pie."   불완전한 문장

The cat had its head **half-buried in a big pie.**   A→B=B'

It noticed and **raised its head** for a moment, but immediately **went** back to the pie.   A↻ and (A)→B, but (A)↻

"This one was for Willy," **Ed said** as he pulled a light pink muffler out of the bag.   A→B

one은 present의 대역이에요.

"Oh... Yeah," **BeeJees nodded.**   A↻

They sat in silence for a moment.   A↻

Snow had covered most of Everville before dawn.   A→B

The snow fell at a steady pace throughout the morning.   A↻

Some wind had started to blow, but **the weather was** reasonably calm.   A→B, but A=B

It was still far from a storm.   A=B

"Well, don't worry," **BeeJees said** to Ed.   A→B

"You already gave Willy **a much bigger present.**"   A→B/B'

p.10

"Maybe," Ed said, a sad smile on his face.　A→B

BeeJees couldn't find anything else to say, so he let his eyes wander off across the street to the old department store on the corner.
A→B, so A→B=B'　　so 이하의 문장은 비지스가 '자신의 눈을 wander시켰다'고 표현함으로써 자연스럽게 거리 저편으로 시선을 두리번거리는 느낌을 살렸습니다.

The building had been closed since the late seventies.　A=B
seventies는 '(19)70년대'를 말해요. 여기에 late를 붙이면 70년대 '후반'이라는 의미입니다.

The doors were nailed shut, the windows were boarded up, and everything else was broken.　A=B, A=B and A=B

"That store there," BeeJees said abruptly.　A→B

"It's just a dump now, but you should have seen it when I was a kid.
A=B, but A→B　　dump는 원래 무언가를 '내버리다'란 의미를 지닌 화살표지만, 거기서 새로 생겨난 의미로 '물건이 버려진 곳=쓰레기장'이란 의미로도 쓰입니다.

Every Sunday, musicians played on that patio.　A⊃
patio는 안뜰에 있는 테라스 같은 곳입니다.

My dad used to take me to see them when he wasn't drunk.　A→B
우리말도 '마시다'에는 넌지시 '술을 마시다'란 의미가 들어 있지만 영어의 drink에도 비슷한 뉘앙스가 있습니다. 이 문장에서는 drunk라는 형태로 쓰여 '취한 상태'를 가리킵니다.

Me and my baby sister each got an ice cream cone from that booth there.
A→B　　baby sister(brother)는 '나이 어린 여동생(남동생)'으로 자기보다 더 어린 동생을 일컬을 때 흔히 쓰는 표현이에요.

They had the best strawberry ice cream ever."　A→B

Ed looked at the patio BeeJees was talking about.　A→B

There were still a few rusty chairs and tables lying around, but it was hard to imagine the patio when it was new.　A=B, but A=B
이 문장에서 hard는 '단단한'이란 의미가 아니라 '어려운'이란 뜻으로 쓰였어요. 무엇이 어려운가 하면 바로 to imagine 이하를 말해요.

It was just like the rest of Ghost Avenue.　A=B

A place left behind and forgotten by time.   불완전한 문장

"Everything seemed to shine in those days."   A=B

BeeJees sighed, but with a smile still on his face.   A↻

"But everything ends, sooner or later.   A↻

화살표로 쓰이는 end는 '끝나다'란 뜻입니다. sooner or later는 '늦든 빠르든' 전체적으로 어찌 됐건 포기해버린 느낌을 주는 표현이에요.

Shops close, towns move away... and people... people die.   A↻, A↻ and A↻

That's just the way it is.   A=B

That은 바로 앞에 나온 비지스의 말들을 가리켜요. 상점은 문을 닫고 도시는 쇠락하고 사람은 죽는 것이 x세상이 흘러가는 way(방식)'라고 말하는 것입니다. 마지막의 it is는 way를 꾸며주는 화장문으로 '그렇게 돼야만 하는 방식'을 말해요.

There's nothing we can do to stop it."   A=B

'Shops close, towns move away ... people die.'의 문장 내용을 'stop할 수 있는 것이 없다'고 비지스가 단언하고 있습니다.

The snow kept falling without any sound.   A→B   p.11

It fell on both the rich and the poor.   A↻

It fell on all things old and new.   A↻

It fell on anything and everything, hiding the world under a soft white cover.
    A↻

"Sometimes," BeeJees said in a sad but gentle tone.   A→B

"Sometimes, we just have to let go."   A→B

let go는 자주 쓰이는 관용구로 '(무언가를) go시키다', 다시 말해 '손을 떼다, 해방시키다'란 뜻이에요. 이 문장에서는 비지스가 에드에게 '손을 뗄 수밖에 없다'고 말하고 있어요.

Ed noticed that BeeJees' voice sounded a little bit like Willy's.   A→B

It brought him some comfort.   A→B/B'

In a peculiar way, Willy had survived, Ed thought.　　A→B

Inside BeeJees.　　불완전한 문장

Inside himself.　　불완전한 문장

Inside them all.　　불완전한 문장

"Some things, we can't change. But some things, we can change. You
　　should know," BeeJees said.　　A→B
　　something은 '무언가'란 의미지만 이 문장에서는 Some things로 두 단어 사이를 떨어
　　뜨린 것으로 보아 단어의 뜻 그대로 '어떤 것들'이란 의미예요.

"You taught us."　　A→B

Ed nodded.　　A↻

After a pause, he said to BeeJees.　　A↻

"I'm going to the mall on the two o'clock bus.　　A=B

　　You know, about the shop in the Food Court."　　불완전한 문장
　　You know는 별다른 의미 없이 '저기, 그게 말이지'란 느낌으로 about 이하를 강조합
　　니다.

"Good idea," BeeJees said, stretching his arms.　　A→B

"Hope everything goes really great."　　(A)→B

"I'm going to decline the offer."　　A=B

"What?"　　불완전한 문장

"I already have a shop here," Ed said.　　A→B

"Besides, they told me I would have to move away from Ghost Avenue if I
　　wanted the shop.　　A→B/B'

Some rule in the health code, they said.　　A→B

And if I rent an apartment, I won't be able to take the cat with me."　　A=B

The cat raised an eyebrow.　　A→B
　　eyebrow는 '눈썹'이에요. 고양이가 '눈썹을 올렸다'란 표현에서 눈꺼풀이 움찔하는 모습
　　을 상상해보세요.

It seemed to know they were talking about it.   A=B
　It과 it은 양쪽 다 cat의 대역입니다.

The empty pie plate from the blueberry pie was lying at the cat's feet.   A=B

"Well, it's your life."   A=B
　이 문장에서의 it은 시간이나 날씨 등을 나타내는 it과 마찬가지로 무엇의 대역인지 확실히 알 수 없습니다. '뭐, 네 인생이니'라고 비지스가 조금 냉정하게 말하고 있습니다.

BeeJees shrugged.   A↺

Ed was about to reply when a voice rang out from above them.   A=B

"Yo! Everything's ready to go, man!"   불완전한 문장   A=B

It was George.   A=B

He had appeared on the roof of the old department store holding the end of an electric cable.   A↺

The other end of the cable was connected to a telephone pole in the street.   A=B

Many of the Ghosts heard George's voice.   A→B

They came out from their usual hiding places into the street.   A↺

BeeJees stood up and gave George a thumbs-up sign.   A↺ and (A)→B/B'
　thumbs-up sign은 엄지손가락을 올려 세우는 동작으로 일반적으로 OK의 의미를 나타냅니다.

"Okay, George. Hit the switch!" BeeJees shouted.   A→B
　Hit the switch도 비교적 자주 나오는 관용구로, 기세 좋게 무언가의 스위치를 올리는 느낌을 지닌 표현이에요.

"Gotcha!" George replied.   A→B

He disappeared behind the edge of the roof.   A↺

The crowd waited in silence.   A↺

Ed stood up too, unable to hide his excitement.   A↺

p.13 Another moment passed in the quiet of the snow, and then suddenly, the roof of the department store lit up with Christmas lights.   A⤴, and A⤴

A loud applause rose up from Ghost Avenue.   A⤴

Everybody yelled "Merry Christmas!"   A→B

George started singing a Christmas tune.   A→B

Within seconds, most of the others joined in, and the street became one big Christmas choir.   A⤴, and A=B

BeeJees and Ed smiled at each other.   A⤴

"It's not anything like the good old days, but it's a lot better than nothing," BeeJees said.   A→B
조금 추상적인 문장입니다. It은 '현재의 상황'을 가리키고 그 상황이 'good old days 같지는 않지만 nothing(아무 일도 없는 것)보다는 낫다'고 비지스가 말하고 있습니다.

The lights were just cheap toy lights bought at the nearest supermarket, and the electricity was illegally pulled from the telephone pole, but the moment was so wonderful that no one cared.   A=B, and A=B, but A=B

After many long years of silence, Christmas had finally returned to Ghost Avenue.   A⤴
미국에서는 Christmas라는 단어에 '사랑과 희망이 충만한, 축복하는 분위기'를 연출하는 신비한 힘이 있다고 믿습니다. 이날만큼은 실제로 기적이 일어난다고 믿는 사람도 적지 않아요. 이 문장의 Christmas도 어딘지 '희망'이 되살아난 듯한 뉘앙스를 담고 있네요.

Standing amid the snow, song, and laughter, BeeJees said once again, softly.
   A⤴   amid는 in the middle of를 줄여 말하는 형태입니다.

"Yeah. Some things... you *can change*."   불완전한 문장   A→B

p.16 "Look, cat," Ed said to the cat once again.   A→B

The cat just frowned.   A⤴

"I told you.　A→B

You can't come with me today."　A⟲

It was ten minutes after two o'clock.　A=B
　　친숙한 시간의 대역 It이네요.

The bus had arrived late.　A⟲

Ed had put one foot up on the step of the bus.　A→B=B′

The cat was just below Ed, looking up at him with an annoyed expression.
　　A=B

It was mad because Ed was blocking its rightful path.　A=B

"You have to stay here.　A→B

I'll be back soon."　A=B

The cat snarled.　A⟲

It was tired of Ed blocking its way, so it decided to get on the bus.
　　A=B, so A→B

"Shut the door! Please!" Ed yelled to the bus driver.　A→B

"What?" the bus driver replied in a frustrated tone.　A→B

The cat was about to jump on the bus.　A=B

"Shut the door, now!" Ed repeated.　A→B

The driver finally pulled the door lever, grumbling to himself.　A→B
　　grumble과 비슷한 단어로 mumble(우물우물 말하다)이 있지만, grumble이 더 거친
　　느낌으로 주위에 들릴 정도로 투덜거리는 느낌입니다. 이에 비해서 mumble은 들릴 듯
　　말 듯한 목소리로 중얼거리는 것을 가리킵니다.

The door slammed shut just as the cat was getting ready to leap.　A⟲
　　slammed shut은 '철컥하고 소리를 내면서 문이 닫히는 상황'을 말합니다. leap은 '도약
　　하다'라는 뜻이지만, jump가 일반적으로 위로 뛰어오르는 것을 가리키는 데 반해 leap
　　은 수평으로 뛰어오르는 경우에 사용합니다.

The cat's eyes widened as it watched the door close.　A⟲

It became angry when it saw Ed standing on the other side of the door.   A=B

p.17

The cat kept its eyes on Ed as the bus started to drive away.   A→B=B'

Ed tried to say something to the cat, but the door was too thick.
    A→B, but A=B

From inside the bus, Ed watched the cat grow smaller and smaller in the
    distance as the bus hurried down the street.   A→B=B'

The cat was still looking at him when the bus rounded a corner several
    seconds later.   A=B

An absurd question suddenly popped into Ed's head.   A↺

What if I never see that cat again?   A→B

He frowned and shook it off immediately.   A↺ and (A)→B
    이 문장에서 shook off(흔들어 떨어뜨리다)한 것은 앞 문장에 나왔던 absurd question
    입니다.

Of course I'll see the cat again. Why not?   A→B   불완전한 문장

But all during the bus ride to the New Mall, the image of the cat sitting there
    alone on the street came back to him again and again and never really
    disappeared.   A↺ and (A)↺

p.18

The snow was still falling quite lightly when the bus reached the New Mall
    some twenty minutes later.   A=B

As the bus crossed the parking lot, Ed could see the empty space where the
    Pie Festival had been held.   A→B

All the tents and rides were already gone and only a few trailers and trucks
    still remained there.   A=B and A↺

Somehow, it all seemed like one big dream now.   A=B

Inside the mall, it was Christmas everywhere.   A=B
이해하기 어려울지 모르겠지만 이 문장에서의 it도 시간의 대역입니다.

A chorus of Christmas songs greeted Ed, and Christmas lights decorated
almost everything in sight.   A→B, and A→B

The movie theater near the entrance was showing a romantic comedy
featuring a blue snowman.   A=B

There were a lot of people in front of the theater waiting for the next showing.
A=B

A child recognized Ed's face and hollered, "Hey! You're that mustard pie
guy!"   A→B and (A)→B
'소리를 지르다'라는 표현으로 가장 많이 쓰이는 단어가 shout입니다. 크게 소리를 질러
서 무언가를 알리려고 할 때 shout를 쓰지요. 여기에 '화가 나서 외치다'란 뉘앙스가 더
해지면 yell이 되고 이 문장에서처럼 아이들이 별 의미도 없는 말을 큰소리로 떠들 때는
holler를 씁니다. 이외에 비명을 지를 때 쓰는 scream 등도 있습니다.

The child's parents quickly seized him.   A→B

Ed blushed and walked on.   A↺ and (A)↺

This happened several more times before he reached the Food Court.   A↺

A giant Christmas tree was standing in the middle of the Food Court.   A=B

It was decorated with real cookies and candy from stores in the mall.   A=B

Zombie Pies was doing an "Evil Santa Pie-Fest."   A=B
Fest는 Festival의 줄임형이에요. 제레미가 아니라면 생각해낼 수 없는 아이디어죠.

Ed's feet stopped when he saw the vacant storefront in the Food Court.   A↺   p.19

The steel shutters outside the shop were pulled down.   A=B

Ed sat down on a bench in front of the shop.   A↺

It was the same bench he had sat on a month before. A=B

a month before는 '한 달 전', the same bench는 〈Big Fat Cat Goes To Town〉에서 에드가 앉았던 bench를 말합니다.

As he looked at the vacant shop, the idea that perhaps everything had been a dream came back to him again. A⤴

that에서 dream까지는 idea의 구체적인 내용을 뜻합니다.

This can't be real. A=B

This는 '이 상황'을 가리키는 대역이고요.

Maybe I fell asleep on the bench that day, and had a long, long dream.

A⤴, and (A)→B   that day는 한참 전 이 벤치에 앉았던 날을 가리킵니다.

Maybe I'm still on that bench... A=B

For some reason, the thoughts reminded Ed of the paper inside Willy's fortune cookie. A→B/B'

He dug into his pocket and found it. A⤴ and (A)→B

6권 마지막에서 포춘 쿠키를 쪼개어 읽었던 쪽지를 에드는 아직도 가지고 있었네요. 그 쪽지에 담긴 의미는……?

It still said the same thing. A→B

It은 paper의 대역입니다. said는 '(종이가) 말하고 있다=쓰여 있다'란 의미로 쓰였습니다. '여전히 같은 말이 쓰여 있어서' 이상하게 여긴 모양이지만. 이 문장에서는 쪽지에 담긴 깊은 의미를 미처 파악하지 못한 채 아직도 처음에 읽을 때와 '같은 의미로 받아들였다'는 뜻이에요.

Most treasures are in the places you first find them. A=B

them은 treasures의 대역이에요. you first find them은 places를 꾸며주는 화장문으로 '(보물을) 처음에 발견한 곳'을 말합니다.

Ed raised his head to look at the shop again. A→B

Then, he read the words once more. A→B

...in the places you first find them. 불완전한 문장

It was almost as if Willy was congratulating him. A=B

He knew that wasn't possible, but for a moment, Ed actually believed that it

might be.　A→B, but A→B

첫머리의 that과 뒷부분의 it은 둘 다 앞 문장 전체를 가리키는 대역이에요. 뒷부분은 Ed actually believed that it might be possible에서 possible을 생략한 것입니다.

p.20

"Ed! Ed Wishbone!　불완전한 문장　불완전한 문장

I'm so glad you came."　A=B

Ed's heart skipped a beat when the owner suddenly patted him on the shoulder.　A→B

He was so absorbed in his thoughts that he hadn't realized the owner was standing right beside him.　A=B that A→B

Ed quickly folded the fortune paper and slid it back into his pocket.
　A→B and (A)→B

"Sir. Good afternoon," Ed said, standing up from the bench.　A→B

"Did the snow give you any trouble?"　A→B/B'

The owner asked Ed in his usual joyous tone.　A→B

"I sure hope not.　A→B

오너는 바로 앞에 나온 자신의 대화문에 대해서 '그렇지 않기를 바란다'고 말하고 있어요.

Now come with me and I'll show you your new shop."　(A)↺ and A→B/B'

"Uh... sir, I..."　불완전한 문장

Ed tried to speak, but the owner went straight to the closed shutters.
　A→B, but A↺

Ed hurried after him, still not sure how to explain.　A↺

"Just a second, while I open this shutter here..." the owner said, turning a key in the lock.　A→B

"Sir. I'm sorry.　불완전한 문장　A=B

I have something to..."　A→B

말을 끝까지 했다면 B 상자는 something to tell you가 됐을 거예요.

Ed felt his stomach tighten.   A→B=B'
본래 tighten은 수도꼭지 등을 '꽉 잠글 때' 쓰는 화살표입니다. 이 문장에서는 stomach(배)에 쓰였으므로 에드의 배가 tighten해졌다는 느낌이 들 정도로 긴장했다는 의미입니다.

He imagined what the owner would say when he told him he didn't want the shop.   A→B
에드가 imagine한 내용은 'he didn't want the shop이라고 owner에게 말했을 때 owner가 뭐라고 말할 것인가' 하는 거예요.

But if he was going to say it, now was his only chance.   A=B
it은 앞 문장의 he didn't want the shop을 가리키는 대역입니다.

"Here we go," the owner said, and threw open the shutters.
A→B, and (A)→B   Here we go는 대중적인 표현으로 연령과 성별에 관계없이 쓰여요. 특히 동료끼리 '자, 가자'라고 말을 건넬 때 쓰입니다. threw open the shutters는 '셔터를 열린 상태로 threw(방치하다)했다'라는 의미입니다.

p.21

The shutters rolled away, revealing an elegant counter with an open kitchen behind it.   A↺

The owner turned on the lights and waved his hand towards the inside of the shop.   A→B and (A)→B

"Well?"   불완전한 문장

Ed was speechless.   A=B

His eyes were wide open.   A=B

The owner noticed this and smiled.   A→B and (A)↺
this는 앞 문장 전체를 가리키는 대역이에요.

He grabbed Ed's arm and pulled him inside.   A→B and (A)→B

"C'mon inside.   (A)↺

Take a look."   (A)→B

Ed walked into the shop in a daze.　A↺

"Wow..." he whispered.　A→B

Everything in the shop looked perfect.　A=B

"The last tenant was a pastry shop. They left everything behind... so you can open your shop at any time," the owner explained.　A→B

Ed nodded, but he wasn't really hearing any of the words.　A↺, but A=B

"Is that the kitchen?" Ed asked.　A→B

"It sure is."　A=(B)
> 앞 문장에 나온 에드의 질문에 대한 답이에요. 원래는 It sure is the kitchen입니다.

"Can I take a look?"　A→B

"Of course you can.　A↺

　　It's your kitchen."　A=B

The owner stepped aside, and Ed moved into the kitchen.　A↺, and A↺ p.22

Hidden behind the beautiful glass counter were countless pots and pans, kitchen utensils, and spice jars.　A=B

Ed touched the counter.　A→B

He stroked its surface softly.　A→B

It was smooth and spotless.　A=B

"This... is all mine?"　A=B
> This는 '여기 있는 모든 것'을 일컬어요.

"Yes," the owner replied.　A→B

"All you have to do is sign the contract."　A=B
> 에드가 해야만 하는 일은 sign the contract이겠지요.

Ed finally recovered his voice, but now, he wasn't sure what to say.

A→B, but A=B

He took a long deep breath and said to the owner, "I have to tell you something."　A→B and (A)→B

The owner smiled his jolly smile.　A→B

"Sure. Anything."　불완전한 문장　불완전한 문장

p.23 "I..."　불완전한 문장

I can't accept this prize.　A→B

I already have a shop.　A→B

Ed tried to say, but the words wouldn't come out.　A→B, but A⊃

The place of his dreams surrounded him in all its hope and splendor.　A→B
　　its는 The place of his dreams의 대역이에요. '꿈의 장소'라고 할 만큼 멋진 가게를 갖
　　게 되리라는 hope와 splendor에 휩싸여 에드는 거절을 못하고 맙니다.

Ed's voice trembled as he finished the sentence.　A⊃

"I... uh... thank you.　A→B

　　Thank you for everything."　(A)→B

"My pleasure," the owner said, laughing.　A→B

"I'm looking forward to having your pie with lunch everyday."　A=B

The owner handed Ed a contract from his coat pocket and patted him on the shoulder.　A→B/B' and (A)→B

"Just sign that and bring it to my office before Wednesday.
　　(A)→B and (A)→B　　that도 it도 contract의 대역이에요.

See you then."　(A)→B
　　then은 '나중에 에드가 contract를 가지고 사무실을 방문할 때'를 말합니다.

Ed couldn't help staring at the contract.　A→B

When he finally raised his head, the owner was already gone.　A=B

He was there alone with the contract.　A=B
　　there는 '그곳=가게 안'의 대역이지만, '그곳에 (혼자) 있다'는 사실을 강조하기 위해 쓰인 것입니다.

Ed closed his eyes tight.　A→B

He hated himself.　A→B

He realized he had completely forgotten about Ghost Avenue for the past few minutes.　A→B

"So the little youngster wants Evil Santa, huh?"　A→B

p.24
　　어른이 아이를 부를 때 쓰는 youngster는 '어리다'는 사실을 강조한 표현이지만, 부정적인 뉘앙스는 별로 없습니다. 좀 더 존중하는 느낌으로 부를 때는 young man, young lady, 낮춰 부를 때는 kid, brat 등을 사용합니다.

Jeremy stood behind the Zombie Pies counter with red and purple makeup on his face, grinning down at a half-scared, half-happy boy who was waiting for his pie.　A↻
　　긴 문장이지만 대부분 화장문이에요. behind에서 counter까지는 '장소'에 해당하는 부록이고, 그 이하는 '어떻게'에 해당하는 부록입니다.

"Well, Evil Santa wants you too!"　A→B

Jeremy suddenly raised his voice and a Santa head with a wicked smile popped up from under the counter.　A→B and A↻
　　wicked는 원래 '악의에 찬'이란 의미지만 판타지나 동화 등에 자주 쓰이면서 현재는 두려움보다는 오히려 익살스런 이미지가 강해졌어요. 정말로 악의에 찬 상황을 표현할 때는 일반적으로 evil을 씁니다.

The child and his mother both screamed.　A↻

So did Ed.　A→B

Louder.　불완전한 문장
　　줄이지 않고 쓴다면 Ed screamed louder입니다.

"AAAGGGHHHH!" 불완전한 문장

Jeremy was shaken by the scream.　A=B

He stared at Ed in dumb surprise.　A→B

Ed had been watching from behind the mother and child.　A=B

Their eyes met as Ed turned red with embarrassment.　A⤺

"Oh, it's you," Jeremy said with a sigh.　A→B
　　it's you는 상대의 인기척을 느끼다가 모습이 드러났을 때 자주 쓰는 표현으로 '뭐야, 너
　　였어'라는 의미예요.

He pulled a rope and the Evil Santa disappeared.　A→B and A⤺

"*That* was scary," Ed said, slowly recovering from the shock.　A→B

"If you think that was scary, go use the men's room.　(A)⤺(A)→B
　　언뜻 보면 화살표 두 개가 늘어선 듯 보이지만, go and use the men's room에서 and
　　가 생략된 거예요. '가서 ~하고 와라'라고 말할 때 강조를 하기 위해 and를 생략하는 경
　　우가 종종 있습니다.

You'll be screaming for the rest of the day."　A=B

"Uh... no thank you," Ed said and pointed at the Slime Bucket Pies displayed
　　under the counter glass.　A→B and (A)→B

"But can I get one of those pies?"　A→B

Jeremy frowned but mumbled "Sure," and reached under the counter.
　　A⤺ but (A)→B and (A)→B

He brought out an empty crust shaped like a bowl, and poured a dip of mint
　　slime into the crust.　A→B, and (A)→B

He handed it to Ed with a wooden spoon.　A→B

Ed took a taste and almost immediately said, "This is great!"
　　A→B and (A)→B

Jeremy just shrugged.   A⤴

"This is the best chocolate mint pie I've ever had," Ed repeated.   A→B

I've ever had는 chocolate mint pie를 꾸며주는 화장문입니다.

Jeremy thought Ed was being sarcastic, but Ed really seemed to mean it.

A→B, but A=B

it은 앞 문장에 나온 에드의 대화문을 가리키는 대역이에요. mean은 '의미하다'로 이 문 장에서는 'it을 의미하다' 다시 말해 '진심으로 말하고 있다'란 뜻입니다.

Too bad for Wishbone,* he thought, *because by the time he opens his shop, Zombie Pies will be gone.   A→B

Too bad는 '지나치게 나쁘다' 다시 말해 '너무 안됐다'란 의미가 담긴 표현이에요. 누군 가에게 불행이 찾아왔을 때 위로하는 표현으로 자주 들을 수 있습니다. 이 문장에서는 because 이하가 너무 안됐다는 뜻입니다.

This was his shop's last week.   A=B

This는 This week의 줄임형이에요.

Jeremy's father had sold the shop to the Everville Rehabilitation Project.

A→B

But he didn't tell this to Ed.   A→B

이 this는 앞 문장 전체를 가리키는 대역입니다.

"You are one strange person," Jeremy mumbled, but not in a bad tone.

A→B   보통은 a를 붙여서 a strange person이라고 쓰지만 one을 써서 '유일한 존재' 라는 것을 강조했습니다.

"Oh, yeah... do you remember my bodyguard?"   A→B

"Sure," Ed said rather uneasily.   A→B

"Of course."   불완전한 문장

"He was arrested this morning."   A=B

"He was?"   A=(B)

"The arrest wasn't a surprise.   A=B

　　He did a lot of *stuff* for my father."   A→B

Jeremy said the word 'stuff' in a disgusted way.   A→B

"The real surprise was that the police were able to catch him.   A=B

He's not an easy man to catch, you know.   A=B
you know는 별 의미 없이 쓰인 상용구예요.

I think maybe he wanted to get caught."   A→B

"Why?" Ed asked.   A→B

Jeremy shrugged again.   A↻

He also knew that if Billy Bob was caught, his father's arrest was not far
away, but that was another thing he didn't tell Ed.   A→B, but A=B
if에서 쉼표까지는 '만약 ~라면'의 뜻인데, 빌리 밥이 붙잡혔다면 자신의 아버지가 체포
될 날도 'far away하지 않았다'는 사실을 제레미는 잘 알고 있는 듯합니다. 두 번째 that
은 바로 앞부분에 나온 문장 전체를 가리키는 대역입니다.

p.26

"Beats me.   (A)→B
Beats me도 매우 대중적인 관용구 표현입니다. Beat은 '(상대를) 패배시키다'라는 의미
이며 Beats me는 '자신을 패배시키다 → 굴복하다' 다시 말해 '모르겠다'란 뉘앙스예요.

I just think so.   A→B
so는 제레미가 '빌리 밥은 붙잡히길 바랐다'고 말한 대화문을 가리키는 대역이에요.

He didn't like his job very much."   A→B

As an afterthought, Jeremy added, "He grew up on Ghost Avenue, you know."
A→B

Ed thought about this for a moment, but couldn't think of anything to say.
A→B, but (A)→B

"So when are you going to open?" Jeremy asked, pretending not to look very
interested.   A→B

Ed smiled awkwardly for a moment.   A↻

"I don't deserve that shop," he said.   A→B

Jeremy frowned at Ed while serving another customer a slice of pie.   A↺

Ed said again, "It's too good for me."   A→B

"Yeah, yeah. Of course you don't deserve it. Everyone knows that," Jeremy
said.   A→B

"You only beat me and sixteen other bakers!   A→B

Sure, you don't deserve it!"   A→B

Ed realized what he was saying and added in a hurry, "Oh, no no! I didn't
mean it that way... Sorry. I'm really proud about winning the contest! I
really am! But that shop... it's just way out of my league."
   A→B and (A)→B
   mean은 '그런 의미로 한 말이 (아니다)'란 뉘앙스를 풍깁니다. 뒤의 대화문을 색깔
   로 구분하면 I didn't mean it that way... Sorry. I'm really proud about winning the
   contest! I really am! But that shop... it's just way out of my league.
   A→B A=B A=(B) A=B

"I know, Wishbone, I know."   A↺, A↺

p.27

Jeremy seemed a bit angry, but his voice was calm.   A=B, but A=B

"So I'll tell you what you don't know," Jeremy said as he took the dirty spoon
back from Ed.   A→B
   조금 어려운 문장이에요. 에드의 변명에 대해서 I know라고 대답한 제레미는 그 말을 받
   아서 '그럼 이번에는 네가 know하지 못한 사실을 알려주마'라고 말하고 있습니다.

"The only thing worse than getting a chance you don't deserve, is wasting
that chance."   A=B

Ed fell silent.   A↺

Jeremy stuck his palm out to Ed.   A→B

Ed didn't understand why and just stared at Jeremy's palm for a moment.
   A→B and (A)→B   에드가 understand하지 못한 것은 Jeremy가 palm을 내민 그
   이유였어요.

125

"$2.55 for the pie," Jeremy said flatly.   A→B

"Oh... sorry."   불완전한 문장

Ed fumbled in his pocket and pulled out three dollar-bills in a hurry.
A⤴ and (A)→B
fumbled는 무언가를 허둥지둥 더듬거리며 찾는 모습을 말합니다. '서투르다', '실수하다'란 의미도 있어서 에드처럼 덜렁대는 사람을 묘사할 때는 꼭 등장하는 화살표예요.

"Thank you very much."   (A)→B

Jeremy took the money and reached under the counter for change.
A→B and (A)→B   change는 '바꾸다'라는 뜻으로 쓰일 때가 많지만 이 문장에서는 '거스름돈'이란 의미로 쓰였어요.

"Here's your change," he said and squeezed green slime out from his hand
into Ed's palm.   A→B and (A)→B

"AAAAAAGHHHHHH!"   불완전한 문장

This scream was even louder.   A=B

p.28

The six o'clock bus was the last bus, but Ed decided to take the five o'clock
bus home.   A=B, but A→B

This turned out to be a very good idea, because once the sun set, the snow
and wind rapidly grew stronger.   A⤴, because A⤴
This는 앞 문장 전체를 가리키는 대역입니다. turn out은 '결과적으로 ~라고 판명이 나다'라는 의미가 담긴 표현이에요. '한참을 turn하고 나서야 비로소 out했다(밖으로 끌어내다)'란 이미지를 그릴 수 있다면 그 느낌을 알게 될 거예요.

When Ed got off the bus, the snow on the ground was already up to his
ankles.   A=B

It was only a short walk back to the theater, but it took him nearly ten
minutes to reach the entrance.   A=B, but A→B/B'
short walk는 극장까지 가는 데 시간이 얼마 걸리지 않는다는 뜻이에요. 두 번째 it은 short walk를 가리키는 대역으로 이 짧은 거리가 실제로 몇 분 걸렸는지 설명하고 있습니다.

*"Reporting live from the New Everville Mall, **this is Glen Hamperton** bringing you coverage of the Christmas celebration events scheduled for tonight."*
A=B   쉼표 뒷부분의 this is Glen Hamperton에서 this is란 표현은 리포터가 중계를 시작하면서 자기소개 등을 할 때 자주 쓰입니다.

The voice from the radio greeted Ed as he closed the door against the snow.
A→B

Ed followed the sound of the radio across the lobby, and into the main theater.   A→B

George was the first one to notice Ed's return.   A=B

"Yo, Ed.   불완전한 문장

You made it just in time, man.   A→B
made it은 '그것을 완성시켰다' 다시 말해 '성공했다'란 의미로, 이 문장에서는 폭설이 내리기 전에 잘 '도착했다'라는 뜻이에요. in time은 '시간 내에(제시간에)'입니다.

We were getting kinda worried."   A=B

"Sorry," Ed said as he brushed the snow from his head and shoulders.   A→B

"The snow's getting worse by the minute."   A=B

George, BeeJees, Paddy, Frank, and a few other Ghosts were huddled around the campfire.   A=B

Frank was holding his new radio in his lap with the volume turned up.   A=B

"We were listening to the radio," BeeJees said.   A→B

"They're doing live from the mall."   A=B
live는 live broadcast에서 broadcast가 생략된 표현으로 '생중계'란 의미예요.

Ed nodded and smiled.   A↺ and (A)↺

Glen Hamperton continued to talk.   A→B

She was introducing a local choir group.   A=B

George got up and went to the large, steaming pot that sat beside the
    campfire.   A↺ and (A)↺

He grabbed a tin cup and dipped it into the pot.   A→B and (A)→B

"C'mon, man. We made you some stew," he said to Ed.   A→B

Ed sat down beside BeeJees and took the cup from George.   A↺ and (A)→B

Warm, homemade stew with large chunks of vegetables.   불완전한 문장

It was perfect for a day like this.   A=B

"So you gave them the bad news?" BeeJees asked as Ed sipped some stew
    from the cup.   A→B

Ed paused for a moment to shake his head.   A↺

"I couldn't.   A→(B/B')
    원래 문장은 I couldn't give them the bad news입니다.

    I'm planning to go back tomorrow."   A=B

BeeJees nodded silently.   A↺

The radio had started to broadcast a Christmas chorus.   A→B

p.30   "Cat, cat, cat. Fat, fat, fat," Frank sang along with his own words.   A→B
    his own words는 '자신만의 언어로'란 의미예요. 프랭크는 자신이 직접 지은 재치 있는
    가사를 흥얼거리고 있네요.

He was singing to a poster he had found somewhere.   A=B
    뒷부분의 he had found somewhere는 poster를 꾸며주는 화장문이에요.

"You got the roof repaired in time," Ed said to George.   A→B

He realized that no snow was falling from above.   A→B

Several wide planks of wood had been laid across the roof, covered with
    some sort of plastic sheet.   A=B

"Yeah. Paddy helped me," George answered proudly, and exchanged a high-five with Paddy.　A→B, and (A)→B

high-five란 두 사람이 손바닥을 마주치는 동작을 말하며, 주로 동료간에 '해냈어!'라며 승리의 기쁨을 나누는 표현이지요.

"Cat fat fat, big fat cat."　불완전한 문장

Ed couldn't help smiling as he listened to Frank's song.　A→B

It was so peaceful here.　A=B

He couldn't believe that it was just a day ago that Willy had passed away.

　　A→B　　passed away는 die, 즉 죽음을 순화한 표현입니다. 영혼이 next world로 passed away했다는 뜻입니다.

Ed knew that all of them were still sad, but everyone seemed to just go on with their normal life.　A→B, but A=B

They had all cried, they had all said good-bye, and now, they all seemed to know that it was time to move on.　A↺, A→B, and, A=B

move만으로도 '움직이다'란 의미지만 move on이 되면 '(off에서) on으로 움직이다'란 의미가 되어 전진하려는 의욕이 더 부각됩니다. 이 문장에서는 윌리의 죽음으로 인해 일시적으로 off된 인생이 '앞으로 나아가야 할 때'라고 말하고 있습니다.

It seemed a little strange to Ed, who had thought that after someone you loved died, you were supposed to be sad for a period of time.　A=B

p.31

It은 '윌리의 죽음에 대한 주위의 태도'를 가리키는 대역이고 a period of time은 '(일정) 기간'을 말합니다.

At least, he had been sad for years, when his mother had passed away.　A=B

— But he liked the attitude here better.　A→B

For some reason, it seemed a lot more natural.　A=B

it은 the attitude here의 대역이에요.

Some things we can't change.　A→B

Ed took a sip of stew as he looked over at Willy's stroller sitting alone by the wall.   A→B

It would probably **stay** there for a long time to come.   A↺

Ed had asked the driver of the silent ambulance where he was taking Willy.
   A→B/B′   ambulance가 환자나 부상자를 운송할 때는 사이렌을 울리면서 달리는 것이 보통입니다. 그런데 구급차가 silent하다면, 결국…….

The driver had answered, "I have no idea."   A→B
   I have no idea는 I don't know와 같은 의미지만, 비교적 정중한 부정의 표현입니다.

It had all been sad.   A=B
   이 문장에서 It은 '윌리의 죽음에 관한 모든 것'을 통틀어 가리킵니다.

But sitting there with the Ghosts, in a town that had a very vague sense of time, **it didn't feel** as sad as it had seemed at first.   A↺
   이 두 개의 it도 앞 문장과 마찬가지로 '윌리의 죽음에 관한 모든 것'을 가리키는 대역. in 에서 쉼표까지는 '시간감각이 무뎌진 마을에서'라는 '장소'의 부록으로, 고스트 애비뉴를 말합니다.

It was just the way it was.   A=B
   the way it was(is)라는 표현은 앞에서도 나왔는데, 'it은 it 방식대로 길이 있다' 다시 말해 '있는 그대로 충분하다'란 의미입니다.

p.32   **Ed felt the warmth of the campfire** once again.   A→B

He felt ashamed of forgetting, even for a short time, how warm it was here.
   A→B

The gentle taste of George's stew.   불완전한 문장

The flickering of the campfire.   불완전한 문장

Frank's funny song.   불완전한 문장

And the slow, almost frozen sense of time inside the theater...   불완전한 문장

Everything he needed was here.   A=B

He shook his head as he finished the stew.　A→B

What was he thinking?　A=B

He had to be careful.　A→B

He had to think real hard because it was...　A→B

Ed suddenly stood up in alarm.　A↩

His face had become very serious.　A=B

He looked around the theater a second time.　A→B

Finding nothing there, he started towards the lobby.　A↩

"Ed. What's the matter?"　불완전한 문장　A=B
　　What's the matter도 매우 자주 들을 수 있는 표현입니다. 'the matter(관심사)가 무엇이냐?' 즉 '무슨 일이냐'란 뜻입니다.

Ed ignored George's question and rushed into the lobby.　A→B and (A)↩

He came back only a moment later, much more pale than before.　A↩

"George," Ed said.　A→B

"Where's the cat?"　A=B

"Mommy. There was a kitty walking in the snow," the girl said to her mother
　　from the back seat of her family car.　A→B
　　kitty는 '새끼 고양이'입니다.

p.33

"What did you say, Jane?" her mother asked from the passenger seat in
　　front.　A→B

"I saw a kitty-cat walking in the snow," the girl repeated.　A→B
　　kitty에 cat을 붙여 kitty-cat이라고 한 이유는 어감이 앙증맞기 때문인데, 의미상 큰 변화는 없어요. 새끼 고양이든 어미 고양이든 어느 쪽에나 사용할 수 있는 호칭입니다.

"Don't be silly, Jane.　(A)=B

　　Look at how thick the snow is."　(A)→B

"But I know I saw one.   A→B

　　It was a big kitty!"   A=B

"It was probably just a fire hydrant or something.   A=B

　　A cat would freeze to death in this weather."   A⤵

The girl looked outside again.   A→B

She knew that her mother was right.   A→B

But she also knew for sure that she had seen a big fat cat walking along the
　　road.   A→B

She had even seen the cat's eyes as it looked back at her.   A→B

"I just hope kitty's alright," she whispered.   A→B

Only the wind answered, with a high shrill cry.   A⤵

p.34　"...the storm has now entered the Spyglass district and heavy snow is falling
　　from the sky.   A→B and A=B

The storm is expected to develop into a blizzard soon..."   A=B

The emergency weather forecast poured out of the radio as Ed, BeeJees,
　　George, and Paddy gathered in the lobby.   A⤵
　　화살표가 poured가 된 이유는 라디오에서 긴급정보가 '봇물 터지듯' 잇달아 쏟아지는
　　상황을 표현하기 위해서예요.

Everyone was covered with snow from head to foot.   A=B

They looked at each other without hope.   A→B
　　They는 그곳에 있는 사람들 전원을 가리키는 대역입니다.

"BeeJees?" Ed asked.   A→B

"Nope. Nowhere," BeeJees answered.   A→B

"George, did you look around the junkyard?"   A→B

"Yeah. It's already covered with snow .   불완전한 문장   A=B

No footsteps." 불완전한 문장

A heavy silence filled the lobby. A→B

Only Frank, who seemed not to understand the circumstances, kept singing the cat song he had made up. A→B

"The mall," Ed said. A→B

"Maybe he came after me." A⤴

지금까지 에드는 고양이를 일컬을 때 it이라고 표현했지만, 긴급사태가 발생한 탓인지 갑자기 he라고 부르고 있어요. 동물을 가리키는 대역으로는 it이나 he 또는 she도 사용할 수 있지요. 역으로 이 중 무엇을 선택하는지에 따라 그 동물에 대한 생각도 파악할 수 있어요. 이 문장에서는 에드가 고양이의 성별을 정확히 모른 채 평소 이미지로 추측한 듯합니다.

Ed checked the only working clock in the theater. A→B

p.35

work는 '일하다'지만 이 경우에는 '정상적으로 작동하다'라는 의미예요. theater 안에 제대로 작동하는 시계가 딱 하나 있으므로 시간감각이 무뎌질 법도 하네요.

"The last bus is due in about five minutes. A=B

I have to go." A→B

George and Paddy looked at each other, then grabbed hold of Ed's arms so he couldn't run off. A→B, then (A)→B so A⤴

가운데 문장의 화살표는 grabbed입니다. 바로 뒤에 나온 hold는 '붙잡을 수 있는 장소'란 의미로 쓰인 배우로, 화살표가 아니에요.

"Ed, man! Wait a minute," BeeJees said. A→B

"I have to find the cat! A→B

He'll freeze to death in this weather!" A⤴

"You'll freeze to death first!" BeeJees shouted. A→B

"If you take the last bus to the mall, how are you going to get back? A=B

You sure as hell can't *walk* in this weather!" A⤴

Ed wasn't listening.   A=B

Paddy held Ed tighter, thinking he was going to run towards the door, but Ed
   was staring at something else.   A→B, but A=B

"Frank," Ed said, blinking his eyes.   A→B

"Frank?" BeeJees asked with a puzzled look.   A→B
   puzzled는 '곤혹스러운'이란 의미로 쓰인 화장품이에요. 이 단어를 배우로 쓰면 puzzle,
   즉 퍼즐이 됩니다.

They all followed Ed's eyes to Frank.   A→B

Frank was still singing his cat song to the poster he held.   A=B

Ed loosened George and Paddy's grips and walked over to Frank.
   A→B and (A)↺

"Frank."   불완전한 문장

Ed started to reach for the poster Frank was holding.   A→B

"Where did you get this?"   A→B

p.36 "Outside," Frank replied with a smile.   A→B

"Good man give me."   A→B
   프랭크의 대화문이므로 다소 문법이 맞지 않습니다. 바로잡으면 A good man gave me
   (the poster)이에요.

"Today?" Ed asked again.   A→B

"Uh-huh."   불완전한 문장
   Uh-huh란 '응, 응'이라며 끄덕일 때 쓰는 단어로 주로 어린아이들이 사용합니다.

Frank pointed happily at the poster.   A→B

"Cat!"   불완전한 문장

BeeJees and George came beside Ed and took a look at the poster.
   A↺ and (A)→B

They held their breath.   A→B

held their breath는 '숨을 잡다' 다시 말해 '숨을 죽이다'란 의미입니다. held란 단어에는 '꼭 잡다'란 이미지가 있으므로 숨이 막히는 순간 등을 표현할 때 자주 쓰입니다.

"Oh no..." Ed whispered.   A→B

Ed grabbed the poster.   A→B

As soon as he read the first two lines, he headed for the door.   A↻

George and BeeJees ran after Ed and seized him just as he was about to step outside.   A↻ and (A)→B

"Let me go!   (A)→B=B'

　I have to go!   A→B

　He's my cat!"   A=B

"Ed!" BeeJees said to him in a desperate tone grabbing him by the collar.   A→B

The weather outside was really dangerous.   A=B

BeeJees knew he had to stop him.   A→B

He shouted in Ed's face, "ED!"   A→B

Ed stopped struggling.   A→B

His face was frozen with fear.   A=B

BeeJees spoke as calmly as he could, "Ed. Listen. Do you really think that anyone can catch that cat? I think... maybe the cat *knew*."   A→B

이 문장에서 비지스는 고양이가 무엇을 알고 있었는지에 대해서는 언급하지 않습니다. 그 무엇은 네 문장 뒤에 나오지만 에드는 이미 눈치 챈 모양이네요.

Ed's face grew stern as he heard those words.   A↻   p.37

"I know it sounds crazy!   A→B

it은 앞에 나온 비지스의 대화문 전체를 가리킵니다.

But... but maybe...   불완전한 문장

Maybe the cat knew that you couldn't take him with you.   A→B

Maybe he left because he wanted you to have that shop in the mall!"
   A⤴ because A→B=B'

Ed lowered his arms.   A→B

BeeJees let go.   A→B

   let go는 '가게 하다 → 자유롭게 하다'. 이 문장에서는 비지스가 에드를 let go했어요.

Ed staggered back a step, not saying a word.   A⤴

He had forgotten about the cat.   A→B

He was so selfish that he had forgotten all about the cat.   A=B
   우리말에서 selfish에 가까운 단어는 '제멋대로'나 '이기적인' 정도가 되겠지만, 영어의
   selfish는 기존의 의미에 '비겁'한 이미지가 더해져 훨씬 부정적인 단어가 됩니다.

He looked around the lobby at everyone's worried faces, then closed his
   eyes.   A→B, then (A)→B

"Damn!"   불완전한 문장

Ed hit his hand hard on the ruins of the ticket counter.   A→B

"What am I doing? *What am I doing!*" he shouted.   A→B

Full of anger at himself, Ed reached into his pocket, took out the contract
   from the New Mall, and ripped it into shreds.   A→B, (A)→B, and (A)→B

He threw the pieces on the floor.   A→B

"I'm sorry," Ed said.   A→B
   무엇에 대해 sorry한지는 다음 문장에서 명쾌히 밝혀집니다.

And before anybody could move, Ed shoved George back with both hands and
   ran through the door.   A→B and (A)⤴

"Ed!" BeeJees shouted after Ed, but George bumped into him and they both fell down.　A→B, but A⤵ and A⤵

bumped는 '쾅 부딪히다'란 의미지만 crashed 등과 비교하면 부딪히는 강도가 덜한 것을 가리켜요. 차가 crashed했다면 차 안에 있던 사람이 즉사하고 마는 이미지가 연상되지만, bumped는 부상을 입을까 말까 한 정도입니다.

When they finally got back to their feet, Ed had already disappeared into the snow.　A⤵

George and BeeJees stood at the front door of the theater, helplessly looking out into the snowstorm.　A⤵

The snow was no longer a romantic ornament for the streets.　A=B

no longer는 '더 이상은 그렇지 않다'란 의미예요. 지금까지 streets의 낭만을 더해주는 장식품이던 눈이 더는 그렇지 않게 되었어요.

It was now a dangerous enemy.　A=B

It은 snow의 대역이에요.

Behind them, Frank's radio continued to give the weather forecast in a flat, emotionless tone.　A→B

"...the wind has now reached forty miles per hour and it is very dangerous to walk outside..."　A→B and A=B

forty miles per hour는 풍속을 나타내요. 우리식 단위로 바꾸면 시속 약 64km입니다. it은 마지막 부분의 to 이하를 가리키는 대역이에요.

A half hour later, Ed arrived at the New Mall and went straight to the pay phone near the entrance.　A⤵ and (A)⤵

He found the number of the Everville Health Center on the poster and dialed it.　A→B and (A)→B

After the tenth ring, a man's voice finally answered.　A⤵

The man seemed tired and reluctant to talk.　A=B

Ed hurriedly explained what had happened.　A→B

"Yes. Big, dark, mean... It's usually walking around Ghost Avenue. Yes! Yes! That's my cat," Ed cried into the phone excitedly.　A→B

"Have you caught him?"A→B

The passing customers all stared at Ed with suspicious looks on their faces.
　A→B

Ed lowered his voice a little.　A→B

"Yes... near Ghost Avenue... Yes... and did you... You chased him for four blocks!?" Ed shouted into the phone.　A→B

He lowered his voice again after a few middle-aged women pointed at him.
　A→B

"But... but he escaped?"　A↵

Half relieved and half disappointed, Ed took a deep breath.　A→B

The man on the other end seemed outraged.　A=B
　the other end는 '(전화선의) 맞은편'이란 의미로 전화기 너머의 상대를 가리킵니다.

"Yes... yes.　불완전한 문장

　Sir, I'm really sorry the cat ripped your new jacket... yes, and your new pants... and of course, sir, I'll be glad to pay for the belt too, but could you please tell me where you saw him last?　A=B, A=B, but A→B/B'

　Sir? Sir? Please don't hang up!"　불완전한 문장　불완전한 문장　(A)↵

p.40 But the man hung up.　A↵

Ed put the phone back down on the hook.　A→B

He turned from the phone, and almost walked straight into Jeremy, who was standing behind him.　A↵, and (A)↵
　who 이하는 Jeremy를 꾸며주는 화장문이에요.

Jeremy was dressed to leave work.　A=B

to 이하는 dressed를 구체적으로 설명하는 부분이에요. ZOMBIE PIES에서 일할 때 하는 제레미의 분장을 떠올려보면 복장만 보고도 일을 마치고 돌아갈 때임을 쉽게 알 수 있지요.

He had a cell phone in his hand.   A→B

"I thought you already went home," Jeremy said, adding in a sarcastic tone, "Or at least something like a home."   A→B

Ed stared at Jeremy for a moment.   A→B

Then he showed him the poster.   A→B/B'

"My cat's lost."   A=B

Jeremy looked at the poster without much thought.   A→B

As he read the lines, his frown grew deeper, and finally froze into an expression of horror.   Aↄ, and (A)ↄ

He spoke to Ed in a low voice.   Aↄ

"Wishbone.   불완전한 문장

   This isn't good news.   A=B
   This는 poster에 씌어져 있는 내용입니다.

   You could be disqualified for this."   A=B

"I don't care."   Aↄ

"Of course you do!   Aↄ
   원래 문장은 Of course you do care!로 '당연히 신경을 써야지!'란 뜻이에요.

This might be your only real chance in life and you..."   A=B
   This는 '파이 콘테스트에서 승리한 것'을 말합니다.

Jeremy realized that Ed wasn't looking at him.   A→B

p.41

His eyes were glued to a small crowd that was developing at the center of the mall.   A=B

Hie eyes란 에드의 eyes를 가리킵니다.

**The reporter, Glen Hamperton, was in the middle of the crowd with a
microphone in one hand.**   A=B

There were also several television cameras moving among the crowd.   A=B
의미가 같은 '~사이'란 단어도 between은 두 사물(사람)의 사이를 오가는 상황을 나타
내는 데 비해 among은 셋 이상의 사물(사람) 사이를 오가는 상황을 나타내요.

**It was probably the program George and BeeJees had been listening to on
the radio.**   A=B
It은 '몰 중앙에서 행해지고 있는 이벤트'를 가리키는 대역이에요.

"Wishbone! Listen to me!"   불완전한 문장   (A)↺

Jeremy grabbed Ed to make him look his way.   A→B

Ed did, but his eyes didn't stop on Jeremy's face.   A↺, but A↺
첫 문장은 원래 Ed did look his(Jeremy's) way로 앞 문장을 받아서 에드가 제레미를
향해 시선을 두고 있는 모습을 나타냅니다.

They stopped on the cell phone he was holding.   A↺
They는 his(Ed's) eyes를 가리키는 대역이고, he는 Jeremy의 대역이에요.

An idea had come to his mind.   A↺
일반적으로는 '에드가 idea를 생각해냈다'라고 써야 하지만 반대로 idea가 '다가왔다'고
표현함으로써 어떤 생각이 퍼뜩 떠오를 때의 느낌을 전달했습니다.

"Wishbone! I said..."   불완전한 문장   A→(B)

**"I have to borrow this," Ed said, and without waiting for an answer, took the
phone from Jeremy's hand.**   A→B, (A)→B

**Jeremy opened his mouth wide in annoyance as he watched Ed examine the
phone.**   A→B

"Is this the number for the phone?"   A=B
this는 다음 문장에 나온 the phone number taped on the side with cellophane tape
의 대역이에요. 비즈니스맨인 제레미는 수많은 휴대전화 번호를 일일이 기억할 수 없겠죠.

**Ed asked Jeremy, showing him the phone number taped on the side with
cellophane tape.**   A→B

"Yes. I have so many phones that..."   불완전한 문장   A→B

"Thanks," Ed said and ran off towards the crowd of people.   A→B and (A)↺

"Wishbone! Hey, wait a minute!   불완전한 문장   (A)↺

   Damn it!"   (A)→B   Damn it은 '젠장'이라는 의미를 지닌 관용구입니다.

It took another moment for Jeremy to sigh and run after Ed.   A→B   p.42
   It은 to sigh 이하를 가리키는 대역이에요.

By the time Jeremy arrived at the edge of the crowd, Ed was squeezing
   between people, trying to get to the stage in the middle.   A=B

Jeremy bit on his lower lip.   A→B

"Wishbone... What the hell are you doing?"   불완전한 문장   A=B

Jeremy followed after Ed but was blocked by a group of teenagers who
   wanted to shake his hand.   A↺ but (A)=B
   who 이하는 teenagers를 꾸며주는 화장문입니다.

Jeremy fought them off, but by the time he escaped, Ed had already climbed
   onto the stage.   A→B, but A↺

Guards came forward to stop him, but Glen Hamperton recognized Ed
   immediately.   A↺, but A→B

"Look who we have here, everyone!   (A)→B
   '우리가 여기서 가질 누구'는 '누가 여기로 오는지'란 뜻이에요. 생각지도 못한 에드의 등
   장에 리포터도 놀란 모양이에요.

   The winner of the state pie contest, Ed Wishbone!"   불완전한 문장

The crowd cheered, thinking Ed was a guest on the show.   A↺

Ed ignored them and went straight towards Glen.   A→B and (A)↺

"Well, what brings you here today, Ed?"   A→B

Glen pointed the microphone towards Ed.　　A→B

p.43

"I'm sorry," was all Ed said before he took the microphone from Glen's hand.
　　A=B

Glen stared in pure surprise as Ed stepped in front of her to face directly into
　　the camera.　　A↺

"I'm sorry to interrupt. But this is something very important to me," Ed said,
　　his voice shaking with urgency.　　A→B
　　this는 '지금부터 하려는 말'을 가리키는 대역이에요.

The crowd around the stage heard the serious tone in his voice.　　A→B

The cheering and shouting died down.　　A↺

Ed took a deep breath and held the poster up to the camera.
　　A→B and (A)→B

"My cat is lost in the snow somewhere," he said as the camera focused on
　　the poster.　　A→B

"I need your help. Everyone's help."　　A→B　　불완전한 문장

In that one moment, the picture of the cat was broadcast to every house in
　　Everville.　　A=B

Snowed-in families sitting in their living rooms watching television all moved
　　closer to the screen to get a better look.　　A↺
　　Snowed-in이란 '눈 때문에 (안에) 갇혔다'란 의미를 나타내는 화장품이에요.

The owner of the New Mall happened to be watching television in his office
　　with a beer in hand.　　A→B

He sprayed his beer all over his desk when he saw the poster.　　A→B

Jeremy covered his eyes with his right hand and moaned.　　A→B and (A)↺
　　moaned는 괴롭거나 고통스러울 때 내는 소리로 '신음하다'예요.

On Ghost Avenue, George, Paddy, and BeeJees all crowded around the radio unable to believe what they were hearing.   A↺

BeeJees dropped his mug on the ground and whispered, "Oh, shit."
A→B and (A)→B

"If you have seen this cat, please call me at 555-22xx.   (A)→B

p.44

This is the cat that ruined the first round of the pie contest yesterday.
A=B   This는 '이 포스터 속 고양이'를 가리켜요.

The health center is chasing him.   A=B

I didn't know any of this until today.   A→B
this는 '고양이가 파이 콘테스트의 first round를 망친 사실'을 가리킵니다.

I'm really sorry, and I'm fully responsible for the situation.
A=B, and A=B

I'll give back all my prize money and disclaim ownership of the shop in
the New Mall as soon as possible."   A→B and (A)→B

Ed looked straight into the camera and said to the people of Everville.
A↺ and (A)↺

"But right now, I have to find my cat.   A→B

That's all that matters."   A=B
That은 앞 문장 전체의 대역이고, matters는 '(에드의) 관심이 있다'는 뜻이에요. all
that matters는 '관심이 있는 모든 것' 즉 '고양이를 찾는 것 외에는 뭐든 상관없다'라고
말하고 있어요.

A silence followed as Ed stared into the camera for a moment.   A↺

Nobody in the crowd moved.   A↺

After taking a deep breath, Ed gave the microphone back to Glen and stepped
off the stage.   A→B and (A)↺

p.45

The crowd remained frozen in position.   A⤴

Ed was sure that everyone was angry at him.   A=B

He didn't look up.   A⤴

But after a moment, a woman began clapping her hands.   A→B

Then a man joined in.   A⤴

A brief pause followed, and then, several other people started clapping their
   hands.   A⤴, and A→B

Ed looked around.   A⤴

He was so dumbfounded that he bumped into a bleak-faced Jeremy as he
   stepped out of the crowd.   A=B

"What the hell was that?" Jeremy asked in an angry voice.   A→B

"I need to borrow your phone for a while," Ed said.   A→B

"Forget the phone, you idiot!   (A)→B

   Do you know what you've done?   A→B

   You just threw away the best chance of your life!"   A→B

p.46   Ed gave him one short nod and headed down the aisle.   A→B/B' and (A)⤴
   one short nod는 살짝 한 번 고개를 끄덕이는 것을 말합니다.

Jeremy followed along, shouting at him.   A⤴

"What stupid reason was that for?   A=B
   that은 에드가 TV 앞에서 보여준 퍼포먼스 전체를 가리킵니다. '(그런 짓을 한) stupid
   reason이 뭐냐'고 제레미가 다그치고 있네요.

   The cat doesn't even have a collar!   A→B

   Anybody would have thought it was a stray!   A→B

   Why did you have to say on TV that it was your cat?"   A→B

Ed didn't slow down for a second.   A↺

He was headed straight outside.   A=B

Jeremy sighed, shook his head, and with a slight change of tone in his voice, continued shouting at Ed.   A↺, (A)→B, and (A)→B

"And what are you going to do without a car?   A=B

Walk!?   불완전한 문장

It's nine degrees below zero outside, you nitwit!"   A=B

It은 날씨를 가리키는 대역이고 nitwit은 '바보'를 비교적 순화한 표현입니다. nit은 '(이같은 기생충의) 알', wit은 '지혜'로, '기생충 수준에 불과한 지혜'란 비유에서 유래된 말이에요.

Ed finally came to a stop by the exit.   A↺

The snow had become even fiercer in the last few minutes.   A=B

The weather outside was so violent that even Ed, despite his determination, had to stop for a moment.   A=B

중간 부분의 despite his determination은 건너뛰고 읽어도 돼요.

"You're really going to choose a cat over a shop in the mall?" Jeremy asked Ed one last time.   A→B/B'

p.47

choose A over B란 표현은 A를 B보다 우선해서 선택하는 경우에 씁니다. 이 문장에서도 cat을 shop in the mall보다 상위(over)에 둔다고 표현함으로써 cat을 선택하겠다는 뜻입니다.

"The cat... *he* chose me," Ed replied.   A→B

"You're so damn stupid, it's almost illegal," Jeremy said, as he pulled out his car keys and headed for the door.   A→B

에드의 고지식할 만큼 착한 성품에 질려버린 제레미가 '그렇게 바보 같이 굴다니 위법이나 다름없다'고 거칠게 말을 내뱉고 있어요.

"You wait here."   A↺

When Jeremy opened the door, the snowstorm noticed, and attacked full
force.　A↷, and (A)↷

Jeremy winced, but stood his ground.　A↷, but (A)→B
stood his ground는 '자신의 땅을 지키고 있다' 다시 말해 '꿋꿋이 버티고 서다'입니다.

The last thing he did before stepping out into the snow was to say to Ed,
A=B　A 상자의 he 이하는 모두 last thing를 꾸며주는 화장문이에요.

"And you better check on that 'he' part."　A→B
에드가 고양이를 he라 부르는 것을 듣고 이런 일에 쓰라린 경험이 있는 제레미는 신경이
쓰였을 거예요.

Ed watched in surprise, as Jeremy dashed through the snow to his car.　A↷

He wanted to thank him, but he had no time to do that now.　A→B, but A→B

The snowstorm had arrived.　A↷

p.48

"Okay folks, I have a message here from one of our listeners."　A→B
본문 48~49쪽에 나오는 대화문은 모두 SRN(Spyglass Radio Network의 줄임형)의
라디오 방송에서 흘러나오는 소리예요.

"Hello, SRN.　불완전한 문장

I'm a college student visiting my grandparents in Everville for winter
vacation.　A=B
B 상자의 visiting 이하는 college student를 꾸며주는 화장문이에요.

It's been a great Christmas for me.　A=B
It은 시간의 대역. Today로 바꾸면 이해하기 쉬울 거예요.

All the family together, delicious homemade dinners, watching a lot of
old movies, a warm fireplace, and a whole bunch of presents!"
불완전한 문장　앞에서 언급한 great Christmas인 이유를 차례로 들고 있네요. 난로
앞에서 정감 넘치는 시간을 보내는 행복한 가족의 모습이 떠오릅니다.

"I have to tell you... Christmas is the best time of year."   A→B... A=B   p.49

Jeremy's black limousine fought through the snow, swerving and sliding, as   p.50
 they drove south on Valley Mills Drive.   A⤵
중간쯤의 swerving and sliding은 fought를 구체적으로 설명하는 부록이에요.

The car routinely skidded sideways off the road, flinging Ed across the back
 seat countless times.   A⤵

He sat up quickly but was soon flung again, and each time he banged his
 head into something hard.   A⤵ but (A)=B, and A→B

"Please keep the car steady!"   (A)→B=B'

Ed cried to Jeremy from the back seat after a fifth encounter with the back
 door.   A⤵

Jeremy, driving with almost zero visibility, shouted back angrily.   A⤵
zero visibility는 '시야 제로'. 제레미가 앞이 거의 보이지 않는 상태로 운전을 하고 있음
을 알 수 있어요.

"It would help if you closed the damn window!   A⤵
It은 if 이하의 행위를 가리키는 대역으로 '창문을 닫아주면 도움이 될 거야'라는 뜻이에요.

 We're going to catch pneumonia!"   A=B

Snow was blowing in through the back window.   A=B

Driving the limousine was even more difficult with snow swirling not only
 outside, but inside the car too.   A=B
not 이하는 snow가 어디를 swirling하고 있는지 구체적으로 설명하고 있어요. 폭설 중
에 창문을 열면 이렇게 되는 것은 당연하죠.

Ed kept his eyes on the roadside with his head poking halfway out the —
 window.   A→B=B'

But it was impossible to spot a single cat in this snow.   A=B
it은 to spot 이하의 대역. a single cat은 '단 한 마리의 고양이'란 느낌으로 폭설 속에 있
는 고양이가 얼마나 연약한 존재인지 강조하고 있습니다.

Ed's lips had gone from blue to black, and he could barely keep his eyes open in the cold wind.   A⤴, and A→B=B'

'입술이 푸른색에서 검은색으로 갔다'란 표현을 이해하기 어려우면 gone을 changed로 바꿔보면 이해하기 쉬울 거예요. 이 문장에서 gone이 쓰인 이유는 '바뀌어버렸다'는 부정적인 변화를 나타내기 위해서예요.

Hope ran out of him with every passing second.   A⤴

Jeremy took a glance at Ed and saw the desperate look on his face.
    A→B and (A)→B

He swallowed once.   A⤴

p.51

"Look, I don't want to sound cruel, but I'm sure you've realized by now that if the cat were still outside, it would already be dead."   A→B, but A=B

you've 이하를 색깔로 구분하면 you've realized by now that if cat were still outside, it would already be dead. A→B

Jeremy took another look in the rearview mirror.   A→B

Ed seemed not to have heard what Jeremy had said.   A=B

"Wishbone!   불완전한 문장

Are you listening, dammit?   A=B

dammit은 damn it을 줄인 표현으로 말을 툭 내뱉으며 '에이, 제기랄'이라고 말하는 느낌이에요.

We could easily die out here too, you know!"   A⤴

Ed bit on his lower lip.   A→B

The big roadside sign for the New Mall stood on the other side of the road.
    A⤴

Everything beneath it was already buried in the snow.   A=B

He knew Jeremy was right.   A→B

They could have passed the cat anywhere.   A→B

His mind told him it was pointless.　A→B/B'
　　it은 '고양이를 찾는 것'을 가리키는 대역입니다.

But the image of the cat sitting there on the street earlier today, and the
　　image of that same cat lying beneath cold snow, slowly freezing to death,
　　wouldn't allow Ed to give up.　A→B=B'

Some things you can change.　A→B

He had to believe.　A→B
　　believe해야만 하는 것은 앞 문장 전체의 내용이에요.

He was so damn tired of losing everything.　A=B

Jeremy's cell phone suddenly rang.　A↺

p.52

Ed fumbled for the phone.　A↺
　　당황한 에드가 주머니에서 휴대전화를 fumbled하고 있어요. 이해하기 힘들면 the
　　phone을 B 상자에 넣고 생각해도 상관없습니다.

It took him a moment to press the talk button with his cold fingers.　A→B/B'

It was a short but horrible moment for Ed.　A=B
　　it은 앞 문장에 나오는 a moment to press the talk button with his cold fingers를 가
　　리키는 대역이에요. 그 순간이 에드에게는 short했지만 horrible한 것이었어요.

He was scared that the caller might hang up.　A=B

"It's probably just another crank call," Jeremy muttered.　A→B

"Hello?" Ed said into the phone.　A→B

"Hello?"　불완전한 문장

There was some background noise, but no voice at the other end.　A=B

It seemed like another hoax.　A=B

There had been five of them already.　A=B

But this time, after a long pause, a small girl's voice came from the speaker.
　　A↺

"I saw your kitty," the girl said.　A→B

"It was walking down Valley Mills Drive.　A=B

Near the big sign for the mall."　불완전한 문장

p.53

"Valley Mills Drive?　Here!?" Ed repeated.　A→B

They had just passed that 'big sign' moments ago.　A→B

"Could you tell me when...?"　A→B/B'
　　when 이후에 생략된 표현은 this happened입니다.

But the phone was already dead.　A=B

The child had hung up, perhaps she was too shy or scared to talk anymore.
　　A⊃, A=B

"Thank you," Ed said softly into the phone and rushed to the window once
　　again.　A→B and (A)⊃

He said to Jeremy, "A girl called.　She said she saw my cat somewhere near
　　here!"　A→B

"And of course you believe her," Jeremy said in a sarcastic tone.　A→B
　　지금까지 상식에서 벗어날 만큼 고지식하고 착한 에드의 성품을 보고 몹시 놀란 제레미,
　　어린 여자아이가 알려준 막연한 정보조차 '물론 너라면 믿겠지'라며 비꼬고 있네요.

ED went back and forth across the car trying to spot something — any sign of
　　the cat.　A⊃
　　전에는 '간판'이란 의미로 쓰인 sign이지만 이 문장에서는 '표시'란 뜻입니다.

Jeremy opened his window too.　A→B

The snow flew through the car now, making the inside of the car almost the
　　same as the outside.　A⊃

They looked and looked, but all they could see was white land.
　　A⊃ and (A)⊃, but A=B

Ed spotted the sign for the sandwich shop he had stopped at.   A→B

〈Big Fat Cat Goes to Town〉에서 에드가 점심을 사기 위해 들렀던 sandwich shop을 말합니다.

He could almost see a phantom image of himself and the cat on the roadside, still looking for a new job.   A→B

Everything that had happened since then — both the good and the bad — the cat had always been there with him.   A=B

then은 '고양이와 함께 이 길을 걸었던 때'의 대역이고 with him은 '그와 함께'입니다.

p.54

The image of the cat lying dead in the snow rose up in his mind again, and he closed his eyes to fight the tears.   A⊃, and A→B

"Willy..." Ed said, almost like a prayer.   A→B

It was the only word he knew that seemed stronger than the despair outside.

A=B   It은 앞 문장에 나온 에드가 말한 대화문의 대역이에요.

And that very name brought something back into his mind.   A→B

that very name의 very는 '바로 (그 이름)'이라는 의미입니다.

The fortune paper.   불완전한 문장

Something told him to take the paper out of his pocket and read it one final time.   A→B=B'

So he did that.   A→B

that은 앞 문장에 나온 B' 상자의 내용 전체를 가리키는 대역입니다.

Most treasures are in the places you first find them.   A=B

And this time, the words made perfect sense.   A→B

p.55

made sense는 관용구로 '뜻이 통하다'라는 뜻이에요.

Ed jumped to the window again and stuck his head out as far as he could.

A⤴ and (A)→B

The snow attacked him fiercely, but about a hundred feet ahead, **he was able** to see the road fork towards Old Everville — towards the Outside Mall.
A→B, but A=B

It wasn't about the shop, **Ed thought.**   A→B
It은 fortune paper에 쓰여진 내용을 가리키는 대역으로 그 내용이 'shop을 말하는 것이 아니었음'을 에드가 깨닫고 있어요.

It never was.   A=(B)
이해하기 쉽게 문장을 바꾸면 The words of the fortune paper never was about the shop이겠지요.

"Turn left at the next corner!" Ed said to Jeremy.   A→B

"What!?"   불완전한 문장

Jeremy thought he'd heard wrong.   A→B

The road to the left at the traffic signal was very narrow and **was** already deeply **covered in snow.**   A=B and (A)=B

It **wasn't** even a road anymore.   A=B

It **was** just a pile of snow.   A=B

p.56

"I need to get to the Outside Mall.   A→B

Turn left at that corner.   (A)⤴

It's over the hill."   A=B
It은 Outside Mall의 대역입니다.

"That corner?" Jeremy shouted, pointing at the nonexistent road ahead.
A→B

"That corner!?   불완전한 문장

You're insane!   A=B

We'll get stranded and die!"   A→B and (A)↺

Ed took a deep breath and calmly said, "Then let me off at the corner."
   A→B and (A)→B

"You're kidding."   A=B

"I'm not.   A=(B)

Pull over by the side and I'll get off."   (A)↺ and A→B
생략되었지만 원래는 Pull over the car by the side of the road로 '차를 길가에 붙이다'
라는 의미예요.

The corner was approaching fast.   A=B

A precious moment passed before Jeremy was able to say anything.   A↺

"Now, wait a minute.   (A)↺

Let's consider this again.   (A)→B
this는 다음 문장 전체를 가리키는 대역. 믿을 수 없는 에드의 제안에 제레미도 이렇게
말할 수밖에 없었어요.

You want me to drive this extra fancy limo *into that pool of snow*?!"
A→B=B'

The corner was now moments away.   A=B

Jeremy caught a glimpse of Ed getting ready to go out into the snow and
   spoke faster.   A→B and (A)↺

"Do you know what this car cost?!   A→B

p.57

The front bumper probably cost more than everything in your bank
account!   A→B

And look!   (A)↺

This new audio system cost something like... damn!   A→B

TO HELL WITH IT!   불완전한 문장

To hell with it!은 자포자기 상태일 때 쓰는 관용구. 문자 그대로 우리말로 옮기면 '뭐든 지옥으로 가버려!'라는 강렬한 표현입니다. it은 '지금의 상황'을 가리키는 대역이에요.

I'M RICH ANYWAY!"   A=B

Jeremy yanked the steering wheel to the left and the car spun off towards Old Everville, crashing head first into the heavy drift.   A→B and A⤴

yanked는 붙잡고 있던 것을 힘껏 잡아당길 때 씁니다. spun(spin)은 '(차바퀴 등이) 곁 돌다'라는 뜻인데 차체가 끼익 소리를 내면서 큰 원을 그리며 돌아가는 모습을 spin으로 표현했습니다. drift는 '떠돌다'라는 의미의 화살표로 쓰일 때가 많지만, 이 문장에서는 '(눈이) 바람에 날려 쌓인 덩어리'란 배우로 쓰였어요. crashing 이하는 '어떻게'에 해당 하는 부록이며 head first는 '머리부터 먼저'라는 뜻이에요.

p.58

"And now the road down to Standpoint is completely cut off.   A=B

All public transportation in the Spyglass area has been halted.   A=B

Please remain indoors until further notice..."   (A)⤴

Frank's radio kept repeating the same message over and over.   A→B

BeeJees, George, and Paddy all sat around the fire, looking glumly at the radio.   A⤴

The wind shook the old theater to its foundations, reminding them how dangerous it was outside.   A→B

바람이 old theater를 foundations(토대)까지 흔들었다는 의미예요. how 이하는 이해 하기 어려우면 how dangerous outside was로 바꿔보세요.

BeeJees sighed.   A⤴

"There's no way the cat could still be alive."   A=B

No one answered.   A⤴

George and Paddy tended the fire in sad silence.   A→B

BeeJees stared at the floor.   A→B

"Uh-uh," someone said.   A→B

긍정을 표현하는 Uh-huh에 비해 부정을 표현하는 Uh-uh가 쓰였어요.

BeeJees raised his eyes and looked at George and Paddy, but both shook their heads.　A→B and (A)→B, but A→B

It wasn't either of them.　A=B

It은 'Uh-uh라는 말을 입 밖에 낸 someone'을 가리키는 대역이에요.

The voice had come from behind BeeJees.　A↺

"Uh-uh,"　불완전한 문장

p.59

Frank said again, smiling his toothless smile.　A↺

He was rolling around in his wagon.　A=B

"What, Frank?" BeeJees said, a little annoyed.　A→B

Frank gave them all a big proud smile and said, "Eddie findie cat."
　A→B/B' and (A)→B　프랭크의 대화문이므로 다소 독특한 표현입니다. " " 안은 정확히 말하면 Ed will find the cat입니다.

They all stared at each other.　A→B

Frank nodded to himself as if he were sure.　A↺

Then he looked at Willy's stroller and nodded a second time.　A→B and (A)↺

With a great big smile, he pointed straight towards Old Everville and repeated in a confident voice.　A→B and (A)↺

"Ed always findie cat."　A→B

The car had run off the road near the top of the hill.　A↺

p.60

It landed in a ditch, one tire buried deep in the snow.　A↺

The engine was still alive, but the headlights were both smashed.

A=B, but A=B

Ed opened the back door of the limousine and **stepped** out into the snow.
A→B and (A)↻

He had hit his head.　　A→B

His right temple was bleeding a little.　　A=B

He peered inside the car to check if Jeremy was okay.　　A→B

Jeremy seemed to be shaken-up, but **he wasn't injured.**　　A=B, but A=B
shaken-up은 뒤흔들리고 난 것처럼 망연자실한 상태를 가리킵니다. shocked보다는 강도가 약한 표현으로 shocked는 아니어도 다소 충격을 받은 상황을 나타낼 때 자주 쓰입니다.

Ed sighed with relief, but before Jeremy could recover enough to stop him, **he started** walking down the hill, straight into the snowstorm.
A↻, but A→B

p.61

The snow came up to his knees, and **it was difficult** to walk even a few steps.
A↻, and A=B

The wind threatened his balance and **the blowing snow suffocated** him.
A→B and A→B　　'바람이 threatened했다(위협했다)'고 하면 이상할지 모르겠지만, 일부러 이런 표현을 써서 강한 바람으로 인해 균형을 잃어버린 에드의 상황을 표현하고 있네요.

But **he didn't stop.**　　A↻

He waded forward, digging through the snow, fighting his way down the hill.
A↻　　wade란 본래 얕은 개천을 걸어서 건널 때 쓰는 단어지만, 눈길이나 수렁을 헤치고 나올 때도 씁니다. fighting his way는 '길과 싸우다'로 걷기조차 힘든 길을 뚫고 나가려고 애쓰는 이미지를 나타냅니다.

His whole body was so cold.　　A=B

His feet seemed like someone else's feet.　　A=B

Down below, he could see nothing but white, white, white land.   A→B

Snow had covered everything.   A→B

He remembered that the Outside Mall was at the bottom of the hill, but all he could see was snow.   A→B, but A=B

Even if the cat were somewhere down there, he had no idea how to find it.
   A→B

But he kept going anyway.   A→B

Halfway down the hill, his legs gave out and he fell forward, tumbling down the hill, creating a long cloud of snow in the air.   A⤴ and A⤴
gave out은 gave up과 비슷해 보이지만 '힘이 소진되다'라는 뜻이며 gave up은 '포기하다'로 느낌이 매우 다릅니다.

He rolled all the way down, and finally stopped after sliding another few feet across flat ground.   A⤴ and (A)⤴
all the way는 '모든 길', 다시 말해 '아주 먼 거리'란 의미예요. rolled와 down 사이에 쓰여 매우 먼 거리를 '굴러 떨어진' 상황을 표현합니다.

He moaned in pain but got up.   A⤴ but (A)⤴

"Caaat!" Ed shouted into the blizzard, but the wind erased his voice.
   A→B, but A→B

He called out even louder, "Caaat! Where are you!? Caaat!!"   A→B

Only the wind answered.   A⤴

Ed was too cold and too tired to think.   A=B

The snow was all around him.   A=B

It came from all directions, completely blinding him.   A⤴

It은 snow의 대역이에요.

His hands were half-frozen and the cold had entered his lungs.
A=B and A→B

He was losing his sense of direction.   A=B
sense of direction은 말 그대로 '방향감각'을 말합니다.

**He knew he was somewhere near the shop, but everything was hidden under
the snow.**   A→B, but A=B

The world was just one big white blur.   A=B
이 문장에서의 world는 에드의 눈으로 본 '세계'를 말해요.

"Cat..."   불완전한 문장

Ed didn't know if he was standing or not.   A→B

He realized he had closed his eyes sometime before.   A→B
sometime은 '언젠가', before는 '이전에'이므로 '(이전의) 어느 시점에서' 눈을 감았었
다는 말이에요.

He was so tired.   A=B

"Cat... I'm sorry..."   불완전한 문장   A=B

Then, everything began to fade.   A→B

Everything became white with the snow.   A=B

p.64   **Willy?**   불완전한 문장

p.66   **"Son, you're going to freeze to death if you sleep here,"** Willy **said** with a
smile.   A→B

Ed got to his knees, thinking vaguely, *you should put on this muffler, Willy.*
A↺

It's really cold today.   A=B

"Willy," Ed said.   A→B

"I'm sorry.   A=B

   I... I was late again.   A=B

   I'm always late."   A=B

Willy smiled.   A↺

"No, Ed."   불완전한 문장

Despite all the wind and snow, Willy's voice was clear and calm.   A=B

It still had that warm tone.   A→B
   It은 Willy's voice의 대역입니다.

"You were never late.   A=B

   You've always made it just in time.   A→B
   '시간 내에'라는 뜻을 지닌 in time은 늘 지각을 면치 못했던 에드에게는 동경의 대상이
   된 단어일지도 모릅니다.

   You found that cat just before it starved to death.   A→B
   starved to death는 '죽음으로 갈 만큼 굶주리다' 다시 말해 '굶어죽다'예요.

   You learned a great lesson just before you gave up.   A→B

   You found the real meaning of winning just before you won...   A→B

   And you saved my soul... all, just in time."   A→B

Ed shook his head.   A→B

"No. I... I... Willy... I've lost my cat...   불완전한 문장   A→B   p.67

I went after him, but I was late again.   A↺, but A=B

He saved me.   A→B

He was always there with me and I was late..."   A=B and A=B

Willy just **stood** there smiling.　A⤴

"No, Ed. **I told you.**　불완전한 문장　A→B

　　You were always there in time.　A=B

　　You just **didn't see it** that way."　A→B
　　it은 지금까지 에드가 지각이라고 여겼던 모든 상황을 가리키는 대역이에요. that way는
　　앞 문장의 You were always there in time을 받아서 '늘 제때에 왔다'는 의미입니다.

"But Willy... I... I..."　불완전한 문장

The moon somehow **appeared** in the sky through the snow.　A⤴

It was the same moon as the one they had seen on the way to the hospital.
　　A=B

It was still beautiful.　A=B

Willy smiled one final time.　A⤴

"You've always **made it** in time... and you **made it** just in time again," said
　　Willy.　A→B

"Now **wake up.**"　A⤴

"Willy...?"　불완전한 문장

Ed opened his eyes halfway and **realized** he had fainted somewhere in the
　　snow.　A→B and (A)→B

He was barely able to get to his knees.　A=B

He looked around for Willy, but **there was nothing** but the snowstorm around
　　him.　A→B, but A=B

"Willy... I..."　불완전한 문장

Ed stopped, noticing that he was holding something in his right hand beneath
　　the snow.　A⤴

He pulled his hand out and **a string came** out from under the snow.

A→B and A↺

He didn't realize what it was for a moment.   A→B
it은 앞 문장에 나온 string의 대역이에요.

He just stared at it.   A→B
이 문장의 it도 string의 대역이에요.

But slowly, very slowly, he realized that he had seen the string before.
A→B

He pulled the string from under the snow.   A→B

A ragged gingerbread man was connected to it.   A=B
gingerbread man은 〈Big Fat Cat and the Mustard Pie〉에서 소개한 ginger(생강)가
루가 들어간 인형 형태로 만든 쿠키지만, 이 문장에 나온 gingerbread man은 플라스틱
장식품을 말합니다.

Ed opened his eyes wider and pulled on the string frantically.   A→B and (A)↺

**A line of gingerbread man decorations popped out of the snow in front of
him.**   A↺

It was a decoration from Pie Heaven's front window.   A=B
이 decoration의 정체는 〈Big Fat Cat and the Mustard Pie〉에 나옵니다. 에드의 파이
가게에 걸려 있던 장식을 말해요. 기억을 잘 더듬어보세요.

Ed got to his feet.   A↺

The storm seemed to have weakened a little.   A=B

Ed quickly tugged on the line.   A↺
끈 상태로 되어 있는 무언가를 양손으로 번갈아 끌어당기는 동작이 바로 tugged입니다.
낚싯대를 끌어올릴 때 많이 쓰이는 단어죠. line은 gingerbread man을 연결한 string
을 가리킵니다.

The other end was stuck under a snow-covered box a few feet away.   A=B
에드가 가지고 있는 line의 '맞은편 끝'이 The other end입니다.

p.69

Ed rushed over to the box and wiped the snow off the top of the box.
    A⤴ and (A)→B

It was his old glass showcase.   A=B
    It은 the box의 대역이에요.

Ed used his hands to find the edge of the case.   A→B

This was the showcase he had always stored his blueberry pies in.   A=B

He pulled off the top of the case and looked inside.   A→B and (A)→B

The snow had penetrated the case, filling up half of its interior.   A→B

Ed dug the snow out with both hands, ignoring the pain in his fingertips.
    A→B

He finally managed to get most of the snow out.   A→B

"No..." Ed gasped.   A→B

Buried under the snow, in a corner of the case, was a ball of fur.   A=B

"Oh no..."   불완전한 문장

The ball of fur didn't move.   A⤴

Ed knelt down on the snow with trembling hands.   A⤴

"Cat..." Ed said.   A→B

The tears he had held back came now.   A⤴
    held에 back이 붙어 있으므로 '붙잡아서 도로 거두어들이다'란 뉘앙스가 있습니다.

He said in a weak voice, "Cat... wake up... please."   A→B

p.70

Ed reached out and touched the body of the cat.   A⤴ and (A)→B

It was cold.   A=B

Ed gulped.   A⤴

A shiver ran down his spine.   A⤴

우리말에도 '등줄기가 서늘해지다'란 표현이 있는데 같은 의미를 영어에서는 이렇게 표현합니다.

"Cat... come on.   불완전한 문장   (A)↺

come on도 매우 자주 쓰이는 관용구로, 'on(점화한 상태)으로 오라!'라며 누군가를 격려하거나 용기를 북돋워줄 때 씁니다.

I found you.   A→B

I found you again.   A→B

This time, I know I'm not late.   A→B

Now wake up!"   (A)↺

From the day it had come into Pie Heaven, it had always been his cat.   A=B

It had preferred his blueberry pies right from the start.   A→B

It was his one and only cat.   A=B

"You can't sleep here, cat!   A↺

C'mon, I wasn't late, damn it!   (A)↺, A=B

I swear I wasn't late this time!"   A→B

절박한 상황에서 자주 등장하는 문구가 I swear입니다. '반드시 ~하겠다'는 열의를 I promise로 전달하기에는 미약한 경우에 쓰이죠. 단 그다지 격식 있는 표현은 아니므로 함부로 써서는 안 돼요.

There was no answer.   A=B

The cat lay perfectly still.   A↺

But somehow, Ed knew the cat could hear him.   A→B

The cat had always come back to him, and it would come back, one final time.
    A↺, and A↺

"C'mon!   (A)↺

I'll bake you all the blueberry pies you want.   A→B/B'

Just... just wake up. Please.   (A)↺   불완전한 문장

CAT! WAKE UP!"   불완전한 문장   (A)↺

But still, no response. No response at all.　　불완전한 문장　　불완전한 문장

All strength began to run out of Ed.　　A→B

> strength는 '강함'이나 '힘'을 나타내는 단어예요. power가 주로 육체적인 '힘'을 가리
> 키는 데 반해서 strength는 보통 정신적인 '힘'이 내재된 '강함'을 표현하는 경우에 쓰
> 입니다.

He stood there a while staring at the motionless body of the cat.　　A↻

It seemed so cold lying there in the snow.　　A=B

p.71 Ed took off his muffler and covered the cat.　　A→B and (A)→B

He bent down and picked the cat up, wrapping it inside the muffler.
> A↻ and (A)→B

The cat's body was still slightly warm.　　A=B

And heavy.　　불완전한 문장

He realized this was the first time he had ever held the cat and it made him
　　cry.　　A→B and A→B=B'
> it은 and 앞부분을 가리키는 대역입니다.

"I'm sorry...　　A=B

I forgot... for a moment there in the mall, I forgot... and you... you probably
　　thought I... I'm sorry, cat."　　A↻, A↻ and A→B... A=B

The cat moved.　　A↻

Ed thought he had imagined it, but the cat slowly looked up at him with a big
　　frown.　　A→B, but A→B
> it은 앞 문장 전체를 가리키는 대역입니다.

"Cat?"　　불완전한 문장

The cat was looking around for blueberry pie and found none.
> A=B and (A)→B

In a very frustrated mood, **it glared at Ed** for waking it up during a perfectly good nap.　A→B

첫머리의 In에서 쉼표까지는 it(the cat)의 상황을 나타내는 부록이고, for 이하는 '왜 고양이가 Ed를 향해 glared했는지'에 대한 설명입니다.

It sneezed once and swiftly **jumped** out of Ed's hands.　A↺ and (A)↺

Ed was completely **frozen** for a moment.　A=B

He stared at the cat with disbelief.　A→B

The cat was taking a stretch as if nothing had happened.　A=B

taking a stretch는 '스트레칭하다'로 고양이들이 종종 보여주는 등을 쭉 뻗는 동작을 말합니다.

"Cat...? **You're...** *okay*?"　불완전한 문장　A=B

The cat yawned.　A↺

Ed reached out for the cat, but **the cat**, as always, **scratched him.**
　A→B, but A→B

"You're okay?!" **Ed said.**　A→B

"Oh my God. **You're okay!**"　불완전한 문장　A=B

Ed closed his eyes tightly as great relief rushed through him.　A→B

It was a moment so unbelievable that he couldn't even breathe for a few seconds.　A=B

He opened his eyes again and **looked at the cat.**　A→B and (A)→B

The cat was still **staring at him.**　A=B

"**I come all this way to find you, and you're taking a nap, you damn thing,**" Ed **said** with a smile on his face, tears in his eyes and snow in his hair.

A→B　you damn thing은 본래 화가 났을 때 쓰는 욕설이지만, 이 문장에서는 고양이가 살아 있다는 기쁨에 에드 입에서 불쑥 나온 '사랑이 담긴 허물없는 표현'입니다. 폭설 속에서도 살아남은 고양이를 발견한 직후에 한 말이므로 thing이란 표현을 써서 고양이를 '사물'이나 '요괴' 취급하는 것도 무리는 아니죠.

p.72

As Ed wiped his eyes, he realized that the snow and wind were beginning to calm down.　A→B

Only a gentle shower of snowflakes was now falling from the sky.　A=B

snow의 이미지는 쌓인 '눈'이나 일기예보에서 말하는 일상적인 '눈'이지만, snowflake 는 아름다운 결정체를 가진 한 송이의 '눈'이란 이미지예요. 하늘에서 떨어지는 눈이 폭 설이었던 지금까지와는 달리 보슬보슬 내리는 눈으로 바뀐 것을 나타냅니다.

"Cat... all during the time I was searching for you, I was thinking why I needed you so much. And I think I finally know now," Ed said as he knelt down in front of the cat.　A→B

대화문을 색깔로 구분하면 all during the time I was searching for you, I was thinking why I needed you so much. And I think I finally know now.
A=B　A→B

A beautiful white world enveloped them as they sat there together in the ruins of Pie Heaven.　A→B

"Mom gave me the recipe, Willy gave me the courage... but you..."
A→B/B', A→B/B'　불완전한 문장

Ed paused.　A↺

"You gave me the reason.　A→B/B'

Even when nobody came to my shop, you were always there to eat my pies.　A=B

You were the one that made me a baker.　A=B

You made me a baker에서 You(=cat)를 한층 강조한 표현입니다.

I would have quit baking a long time ago if it wasn't for you."　A→B

quit baking은 '(파이) 굽기를 그만두다'란 의미. if 이하는 그 이유를 나타내는 문장으로 '널 위하는 게 아니었다면' 파이 굽기를 그만두었을 것이라고 말하고 있어요. 어려운 문 장이지만 굳이 의미를 정확히 따지려 하지 말고 전후사정을 살피면서 감각적으로 의미 를 파악해보세요. if 이하를 if you weren't there로 바꿔도 괜찮습니다.

Ed smiled and said to the cat in a voice that was his most sincere, "Thanks. Thanks a lot."　A↺ and (A)→B

For a moment, time itself seemed to pause.   A=B

The world was quiet and forgiving in the silent snowfall.   A=B
 snow가 '쌓인 눈', snowflake가 '눈의 결정'이라면 snowfall은 '내리는 눈'입니다. 단어 자체에 눈이 높은 곳에서 지면으로 떨어지는 이미지가 있네요.

Even then, Ed knew in the back of his mind, that time would start moving
 again soon.   A→B

He would have to apologize to a lot of people, and he would also have to find
 a way to build a new life.   A→B and A→B

But for now, he didn't care.   A↺

It was only him and the cat — just as it was in the beginning.   A=B

Ed stood up.   A↺

You are a baker, Ed.   A=B

Just a baker without a shop.   불완전한 문장

Now go back. Bake your pie.   (A)↺ and (A)→B

"I will, Willy," Ed whispered to himself as he wrapped the muffler around
 him.   A→B

The cat had become tired of waiting.   A=B

It decided to scratch Ed again.   A→B

"I know, I know.   A↺, A↺

 I'll bake you a blueberry pie as soon as we get home.   A→B/B'

 I have to get the Magic Pie Shop ready anyway."   A→B
 get~ready는 '~이 ready한 상태'를 get하다, 즉 '준비하다'란 뜻입니다.

The cat scratched him for an answer.   A→B

Ed smiled.   A↺

"And cat, you really need a name," he said.   A→B

p.74

The snowstorm had reduced all the colors in the world to a big white land of
snow.   A→B

In the distance, a police siren was coming their way.   A=B

Ed and the cat started walking back towards town, their footsteps lined close
together in the snow.   A→B

This night will end, but soon, a new day will begin in the town of Everville.
A↶, but A↷

p.76

There are a lot of pies in this world.   A=B

p.78

Some are sweeter than others.   A=B
Some are sour.   A=B
Some are even spicy or bitter or hot.   A=B

p.79

But that's not important.   A=B
What's important is that every pie is different.   A=B
Every pie has its own taste.   A→B

p.80

My pie may not be sweet — it may seem funny at first sight.   A=B   A=B
But it's all I have, and it's all mine.   A=B, and A=B

p.81

And whatever the pie... whatever the taste... if you have friends, family, and of course... a cat you love... that pie will always taste good.   A↩

Even if it is... a mustard pie.   불완전한 문장

p.82

BFC 시리즈를 끝내며

드디어 종착역에 도착했습니다. 이 글이 Big Fat Cat 시리즈의 마지막 페이지입니다.

에드와 고양이의 이야기는 이것으로 끝이 납니다. 하지만 고양이와 에드의 인생은 여전히 계속됩니다. 이제 그들의 이야기는 살짝 덮어두기로 합시다.

왜냐하면 고양이와 에드뿐 아니라 누구에게나 인생은 계속되기 때문입니다. 영어를 배우는 것도 계속됩니다. 끝이 아닙니다. 저 앞길에 많은 사람들, 많은 이야기가 기다리고 있습니다. Big Fat Cat 시리즈도 다른 이야기들을 여러 편 읽고 난 뒤에는 초보 시절의 길잡이였던 책 중의 하나로 남겠지요. 그래도 괜찮습니다.

지금 여러분이 서 있는 자리는 영어와 미래의 길이 교차하는 지점으로 기념할 만한 장소입니다. 하나의 이야기를 통해서 우리 스태프와 여러분이 시간을 함께 보낼 수 있었던 소중한 장소입니다. 하지만 여기서 멈추지 말고 저 멀리 앞으로 나아가길 바랍니다. 우리들이 보이지 않을 만큼 멀리, 똑바로 걸어가시길 바랍니다. '영어를 할 수 있다'고 느끼는 때는 결승점이 아닙니다. 바로 이때가 출발점입니다. 영어가 어려워지는 것은 지금부터입니다. 모처럼 손에 넣은 편리한 도구를 종종 활용하시길 바랍니다.

영어는 간단합니다. 처음부터 계속 이 말을 해왔습니다. 이제는 마지막이니 조금 더 덧붙이기로 하지요. 영어는 간단합니다. 그러나 다른 사람에게 진심을 전달하는 것은 어떤 언어라도 어렵습니다. 그래서 형태에 얽매이지 않는, 마음을 담은 언어가 필요한 것이지요. 영어에 마음을 담기 위해서, 부디 언제까지나 영어와 가깝게 지내길 바랍니다.

만약 영어에 싫증을 느끼거나 지겨워지거든 슬그머니 뒤를 돌아다보세요. 그때쯤이면 이미 지평선 너머 저 멀리까지 갔을지도 모르겠지만, 지금까지 걸어온 길 저편 아득히 홀쭉한 청년과 뚱뚱한 고양이의 그림자가 보이겠지요. 그럼 미소를 띠며 추억을 되살려보길 바랍니다. 처음으로 영어를 읽게 되었을 때 느꼈던 그 기분을, 얼마나 기뻐했는지를.

그래요. 우리는 언제나 여러분의 뒷자리에 있습니다.

Good luck and many many happy readings on your journey ahead!
Takahiko Mukoyama

이 시리즈는 영문법 교재가 아닙니다. 학습서도 아닙니다. '영어 읽기'를 최우선 목표로 삼고 쓴 책입니다. 몸으로 체험하고 느낄 수 있도록 기존 영문법과는 조금 다른 해석을 실은 부분도 있습니다. 어디까지나 이제 막 영어 읽기를 시작하는 학생들의 이해를 돕기 위해서 의도적으로 도입한 장치들입니다.

STAFF

written and produced by Takahiko Mukoyama	기획 · 원작 · 글 · 해설 무코야마 다카히코
illustrated by Tetsuo Takashima	그림 · 캐릭터 디자인 다카시마 데츠오
translated by Eun Ha Kim	우리말 번역 김은하
art direction by Yoji Takemura	아트 디렉터 다케무라 요지
technical advice by Fumika Nagano	테크니컬 어드바이저 나가노 후미카
edited by Will Books Editorial Department	편집 윌북 편집부
English-language editing by Michael Keezing	영문 교정 마이클 키징
supportive design by Will Books Design Department	디자인 협력 윌북 디자인팀
supervised by Atsuko Mukoyama Yoshihiko Mukoyama	감수 무코야마 아츠코(梅光学院大学) 무코야마 요시히코(梅光学院大学)
a studio ET CETERA production	제작 스튜디오 엣세트러
published by Will Books Publishing Co.	발행 윌북

special thanks to:

Mac & Jessie Gorham
Baiko Gakuin University

series dedicated to "Fuwa-chan", our one and only special cat

Studio ET CETERA는 야마구치현 시모노세키시에서 중학교 시절을 함께 보낸 죽마고우들이 의기투합하여 만든 기획 집단입니다. 우리 스튜디오는 작가, 프로듀서, 디자이너, 웹마스터 등 다재다능한 멤버들로 구성되어 있으며 주로 출판 분야에서 엔터테인먼트와 감성이 결합된 작품을 만드는 것을 목표로 하고 있습니다.
ET CETERA라는 이름은 어떤 분류에도 속할 수 있으면서 동시에 어떤 분류에도 온전히 속하지 않는 '그 외'라는 뜻의 et cetera에서 따왔습니다. 우리들만이 할 수 있는 독특한 작품을 만들겠다는 의지의 표현이자 '그 외'에 속하는 많은 사람들을 위해 작품을 만들겠다는 소망이 담긴 이름입니다.

옮긴이 **김은하**

유년 시절을 일본에서 보낸 추억을 잊지 못해 한양대학교에서 일어일문학을 전공했다. 어려서부터 한일 양국의 언어를 익힌 덕분에 번역이 천직이 되었다. 번역하는 틈틈이 바른번역 글밥 아카데미에서 출판 번역 강의를 겸하고 있다. 주요 역서로 〈클래식, 나의 뇌를 깨우다〉, 〈지구 온난화 충격 리포트〉, 〈세계에서 제일 간단한 영어책〉, 〈빅팻캣의 영어 수업: 영어는 안 외우는 것이다〉 등 다수가 있다.

Big Fat Cat and the Snow of the Century
빅팻캣과 100년 만의 폭설 빅팻캣 시리즈 7

펴낸날 개정판 1쇄 2018년 5월 20일
        개정판 5쇄 2024년 5월 24일
글작가 무코야마 다카히코
그림작가 다카시마 데츠오
옮긴이 김은하

펴낸이 이주애, 홍영완
펴낸곳 (주)윌북
출판등록 제2006-000017호

주소 10881 경기도 파주시 광인사길 217
전자우편 willbooks@naver.com
전화 031-955-3777
팩스 031-955-3778
홈페이지 willbookspub.com
블로그 blog.naver.com/willbooks 포스트 post.naver.com/willbooks
트위터 @onwillbooks 인스타그램 @willbooks_pub

ISBN 979-11-5581-171-9 14740